IT WAS THAT DANG RED-HEADED PREACHER'S KID!
EPISODES FROM MY WHIMSICAL CHILDHOOD

Shane,
So appreciate our
friendship over the
years. Enjoy the book,
and stay whimsical!
Jim

IT WAS THAT DANG RED-HEADED PREACHER'S KID!
EPISODES FROM MY WHIMSICAL CHILDHOOD

Jim Ed Hardaway

EPICTREK PUBLISHERS

2016

First Printing: 2016

ISBN 978-0-692-65447-7

Epictrek Publishers
12448 Mount Belford Way
Peyton, Colorado 80831

www.DangPreachersKid.com
www.JimEdHardaway.com

Some names of people have been changed as well as their identifying characteristics. For the sake of narrative flow, timelines have been modified or condensed.

Ordering Information:
Books are available in special quantity discounts when purchased in bulk by corporations, organizations, and special interest groups. For details, contact the publisher at the above listed websites or email at EpictrekPublishers@gmail.com

For Mom & Dad

My Tonya

Chase

Caleb

Carson

In memory of Joe

EPISODES

ACKNOWLEDGMENTS

Mom and Dad, there would be no episodes if it weren't for you. I wouldn't have seen the DeLorean Time Machine at Universal Studios Hollywood in 1985, and I might've cut myself running with scissors. And I forgive you for not buying me the 64-count box of Crayola Crayons with the built-in sharpener on the back. You're the best!

My Tonya, I am *STILL* head over Vans for you. I love you more than tacos and my massive 80s memorabilia collection. I know that's hard to believe, but it's true. You are my density.

Chase, Caleb, and Carson, thanks for being so rad and for letting me be your dad.

To all my family, I hope this book is funnier than the time Pam got stuck in the tree, or the time William shouted the s-word as he fell backwards off the edge of the patio in his chair. Thanks for the memories.

To all my friends growing up, here's to the good times.

Virtual high fives to George, Robert, Steven, and John for obvious reasons.

Thank you D'Arcy for lending your talents to this book. I am grateful for your honesty and belief in the creative possibilities. You're working on your book, right?

Thank you Cheryl for looking over every letter to make sure it wasn't upside-down, and for tolerating the dot, dot, dots when there should have been an em dash. I appreciate the time and energy you invested in the project, and for every word of encouragement written in red in the margins.

Chris, your design skills are sick! Much appreciated.

Life is a collection of stories we owe to the people around us.

– J. E. H.

PRELUDE

My childhood was whimsical. I tied a pillowcase cape around my neck and transformed into the superhero Batman to defend the neighborhood against evil villains. That was probably the unsuspecting kid next door with the weird cowlick and mangy dog. Remember him? It was a rare occasion if I wasn't seen with a Star Wars action figure in one hand and a Hot Wheels car in the other. I had holes in the knees of my blue jeans from pushing those cars across the floor, picturing myself as the cartoon character *Speed Racer* behind the wheel of his futuristic race car, the Mach 5, racing towards the finish line. The imaginary crowd cheered from the sofa as Speed's archenemy, the illusive Racer X, scowled in defeat.

As the son of a preacher, I was no different than any other kid, except I had a backstage pass to the communion supplies. I could snack on handfuls of those tiny, tasteless Lord's Supper wafers and collect the little clear-plastic cups to play with later. They made excellent shot glasses for lemonade moonshine.

There is a stigma about preacher's kids, that they're the worst of the worst. Don't get me wrong; I've seen a few PKs who made Miley Cyrus look like Mother Teresa. That wasn't me. I guess I was an exception to the rule, but I was by no means perfect. I stole candy, kissed a girl hiding in the closet at daycare, knocked over most of the neighborhood trash cans on a regular basis, and wrecked at least three cars before my 18th birthday. My cousin and I used to hide in the

1

crawdad-infested ditch and moon passing cars. "Mooning" is when you bend over, drop your pants *and* tighty whities, and expose your naked butt to somebody. We'd scar those poor drivers for life and then run like laughing madmen to hide in the woods.

I have great memories from growing up—from the ginormous artificial Christmas tree standing in the church sanctuary for members to hang their Lottie Moon offerings on to the bright yellow Sony Walkman cassette player clipped to the waist of my shamefully short corduroy Ocean Pacific shorts in high school. I burned more AA batteries in that Walkman than I can count, playing secular music mix tapes I secretly recorded in my closet to hide from the preacher. I just might be personally responsible for sending Madonna's "Like a Virgin" song and Van Halen's "Hot for Teacher" song to the top of the billboard charts—all while being madly in love with contemporary-Christian-music artist Amy Grant! While Van Halen was busy running with the devil, I was busy chasing the devil away. Hell has no fury like a Scripture-quoting preacher's kid. I was storming the fiery pit with a water pistol and taking prisoners.

I've been asked over the years how I stay so energetic and zany in life, and my answer is always the same: I refuse to let society's pressure to be successful steal away my childhood imagination. Sadly, this has happened to so many in the name of adulthood. That's why I still have an Indiana Jones shrine in my office to this day. As the days turn into years and the birthdays come and go, the joy that once was driven by imagination becomes enslaved to obligations. Our "maturing" is really a masquerade, and our disappointments lead to compromise. We put on shows to impress those around us and hide behind masks of unfulfilled dreams.

Now our pretending is no longer about our childhood imaginings, but a rigorous climb to social status.

We all do it. We pretend everything is okay. We pretend to be happy when stressed, in control when under pressure, and advancing when in retreat. At what point in our lives did the change happen? At what point did we relinquish our dreams, and where have the wanna-be superheroes gone? The change happened the moment we felt it was silly to believe in the impossible.

Let's go back in time.

Cancel that next appointment, sit back, relax, and let's rewind the clock. Fire up the Flux Capacitor in the time machine, turn the time circuits on, and input your destination date on the keypad that takes you back to a happy place in your childhood. Maybe it's when you had to go to the doctor to get blue Play-Doh removed from your nose, or when you baked your first Easy-Bake Oven dessert, made your brother eat it, and he barfed all over the house. Oh yea, or how about the time you egged the cars parked at the First United Methodist Church! Maybe it was that day in kindergarten when your best friend dared you to run across the room during the reciting of the Pledge of Allegiance.

I remember it like it was yesterday...

It Was That Dang Red-Headed Preacher's Kid!

This is heavy!

It Was That Dang Red-Headed Preacher's Kid!

PLEDGE OF ALLEGIANCE DARE MASTER

There are just a few things I remember about my kindergarten year. I remember that small colorful classroom decorated with the over-sized faces of famous presidents thumb tacked to the walls and our construction paper artwork plastered in between George Washington and Abraham Lincoln. I remember the smells of Elmer's glue mixed with cafeteria goulash mingled with the poots of every boy in the classroom who held it to the last minute because he didn't want to go Number 2 at school. Without question, the most memorable moment was the time I got a good spanking for interrupting our morning patriotic vows.

Every day, class began with announcements from the loud speaker and the reciting of the Pledge of Allegiance. Our teacher, Mrs. B, would call us to order. The forming of our ceremonial circle was no quiet matter, and Mrs. B shook her ancient pointy finger around in the air like a Civil War musket. We jumped out of our seats and shuffled into position as she picked up the discarded chairs we left behind. Once the circle was formed, we would publicly declare the words together.

On this particular morning, just minutes before our ritual, my friend Matthew whispered a sinister dare into my ear. You know the kind of dare I'm talking about, and you've probably experienced one yourself. A risky challenge from someone to defy all human odds and achieve the impossible, one where you must prove yourself worthy of bravery and join the elite group of playground rebels. Matthew's dare was clear and precise, to run across the fellowship circle, touch someone on the other side, and run back. I would have been a fool to ignore such a stupid dare, only to be mocked by my fellow kindergarteners!

We stood there with our posture at attention like miniature patriotic soldiers, with our right hands held over our tiny hearts. All our little voices began chanting in beautiful unison: *"I pledge allegiance, to the flag, of the United States of America ..."* Somewhere between *United* and *States* I took off in a full sprint, with the theme song of *Merrie Melodies* orchestrating in my head underneath my majestic bowl-cut hair. My classmates watched in awe as I gallantly carried out my mission in self-assured glee. It rivaled Paul Revere's famous midnight gallop through the Massachusetts countryside. I quickly tagged someone on the other side and began my triumphant return to my original spot, feeling victorious. The glory was short-lived.

In the few nano seconds it took me to turn around and start running back, Mrs. B had grabbed her beast of a wooden paddle from her desk. I am still convinced to this day that that paddle was forged in fire from the wood of an oak tree found only in the darkest corners of Sherwood Forest. It connected with my rear in point-blank range with a more powerful swing than Babe Ruth and sent me reeling back to the other side. It was probably the first time in American history that the Pledge of Allegiance was followed by such agonizing choreography, as I gripped both butt cheeks in my hands and hopped up and down in pain. Cheers of mockery accompanied my tribal Dare Dance of Defeat, and Matthew stood there holding his gut and laughing uncontrollably.

Kindergarten

It Was That Dang Red-Headed Preacher's Kid!

IT STARTED WITH A DEVIL COSTUME

It was the biggest surprise I got since leaving the birth canal. I was formally introduced to the strange, quizzical day called *Halloween* when my family visited some friends from my father's seminary. My curiosity ballooned with wonder as my three-year-old-kid-eyes watched the other children in the house adorn themselves in festive, multicolored costumes to go trick-or-treating. What human being with half a brain, or even a lick of common sense, would pass up the most outstanding chance to get free candy from the neighbors?

There was a boy dressed as a masked cowboy, with a red bandana tied around his neck and a fuzzy, coal-black, western hat on top of his head. Skipping around the room was an older girl in a baggy, pastel-striped clown costume. It had puffy oversize sleeves. Her face was painted white with rosy red cheeks and a joker-like smile, and her neck was clad with a flappy, inflated collar with gold trim around the edges. There was an extra devil costume in the house, and the family said I could wear it.

The jury is still out on this one but, to this day, my mother *insists* that the clown-girl had outgrown the devil costume and it was the *only* thing available for me to wear. The preacher's wife dressed me as Lucifer for Halloween! The crimson-red Prince of Darkness outfit came complete with big red horns on either side of the hood and a black pitchfork emblazoned on the chest. I got some face paint too—a long, thin mustache with twisted ends on my tiny upper lip and a black goatee beard scribbled on my tiny chin.

We walked out into the night and began our door-to-door crusade to get candy. The mind-controlling capability these yummy sweets have over kids' brains knows no bounds. How children can meander aimlessly in the darkness among ghosts, witches, ghouls, and spooks of every kind for a bag of free candy remains a mystery, especially since the Ghostbusters weren't around yet. The crazy idea that the only price kids might pay is the possibility of soiling their underwear, because some monster jumps out of the bushes to scare them, baffles the human mind. And that's just what happened.

Some big guy in a hairy gorilla costume scared the crap out of us! The horrific incident made us all scream and cry, and we wanted to go home. I'd like to say that clever ape scared all of "it" out of me, but apparently, there was enough left inside to fuel a dune-buggy ride of comical mischief and misdemeanors for the rest of my childhood. Whether or not it was the stereotypical tiny angel on my shoulder whispering in one ear and a mini devil on the opposite shoulder whispering in the other ear, I'm not quite sure.

My mother's surprising antics might've inspired my high-spirited behavior. There was the time my mom fired a .22-rifle in the garage and killed a "giant rat," which turned out to be a baby opossum. She hadn't shot a gun twice in her life! After a few deadly ricochets the bullet exited through the sheet-metal wall of the garage. Then there was the time when she put the Snapper riding lawnmower on its back end because the handlebars got caught in the tire swing hanging from a pecan tree. That mowing machine twisted around and around and around until it couldn't twist anymore, then popped a wheelie into the air. She hung on like Bud on the mechanical bull in *Urban Cowboy*. There was also the time my mom drove my motorized mini-bike right through the neighbor's chain-link fence!

It was also quite possible that being an only child had something to do with the escapades I found myself in. Let's be honest, the exclusivity of my childhood had its pros and cons. If something was broken in the house, it was quite obvious who had done it, or if trouble was to be found, there was no one else to point the finger at. I couldn't blame it on the dog. The dog wasn't with me at daycare when one of the teachers caught me kissing a girl in the playroom closet. And who would believe that the dog made me pick up the discarded can of Copenhagen laying in the front yard and try a dip? Besides, the mutts I grew up with didn't necessarily have the most convincing names to be deemed agitators. There was Runt, Precious, and then Happy.

Most of the time my irrepressible curiosity was roused by the boundless outdoors. The balmy Texas weather accommodated playing outside almost every day of the calendar year. Although, the scorching sunshine was by far a bigger enemy to me than anything the dismal wintertime weather could muster up. My sensitive, fair-complexion skin burned quicker than a jackrabbit on a date—ten seconds in the blistering sunshine and I was redder than those deplorable radishes my father ate in his salads.

My mother kept a growing collection of Coppertone sunscreens handy at all times. It had to be the waterproof formula in the white squeeze bottle and offer the absolute strongest protection against the suns harmful rays. The fresh coconut scent, vitamin E, and aloe ingredients were only bonuses, not essentials. Every time we needed a new bottle, she'd go to the store to see if the manufacturers had come up with a new SPF level yet. No sun-burning kid on the planet knew what the heck "SPF" stood for, but apparently it was of extreme importance. Mom was currently using an SPF 30 on my delicate epidermis, but she was always on the lookout for an SPF 500+.

Coppertone had the familiar marketing ad of the little tan girl with the blonde hair standing on the beach. It read: "Tan...don't burn...use Coppertone." The poster girl had her head turned back in surprise as a little black dog bit her swim trunks, pulling them down and exposing her white butt. It was fixating. I'd stand there staring at that revealing picture, completely paralyzed with drool dripping from my open mouth until mom caught me and pulled me away. That was about the time my mother decided—on a surprising whim—that I no longer burned in the sun and could get a tan. Let's just say I had to be quarantined indoors after that incident until the swelling went down and the blisters disappeared. I couldn't even bend my arms down because they were burnt to a crisp and stuck out from the sides of my body like wings on an airplane.

From then on, my mother smeared me with sunscreen from head to toe. Until I was a teenager, I couldn't imagine a scenario where my skinny white buttocks might be exposed while playing outside, but in the unusual event that it happened, I was covered and ready to go—even during the Christmas holidays.

The infamous devil costume

It Was That Dang Red-Headed Preacher's Kid!

Jim Ed Hardaway

THE CHICKEN POX CHRISTMAS

There was no snow on the ground that Christmas Eve night, nothing but a wind that whistled through the panes outside my window. I could see the stars through my bedroom curtains. They dangled from the sky just as the colored lights hung from our Christmas tree. I was supposed to be asleep, but my toes wiggled inside my footed pajamas because I was filled with uncontrollable glee. My baby-blue eyes produced a soft glow on the ceiling. Static electricity drew thin strands of my red hair across the pillow, turning my bowl-cut hair into an electric halo over my head. It was a symbol of how nice I had been all year, and Santa Claus was sure to make good on it tonight.

A gentle smile pushed my cheeks aside. My tongue emerged through the space where my front teeth used to be and found a few crumbs stuck to the corners of my mouth from my mother's holiday cookies. She had baked vanilla cookies cut in the shapes of trees, stars, stockings, and candy canes, all glazed with colorful icing, and topped with delicious sugar sprinkles. They were my favorite. I would have happily survived on them all year long, but my childhood was often disrupted with my father's favorite blend of sauerkraut and weenies. Having to eat that detestable entrée was right up there with stepping in a fresh pile of doggy poo while playing in the yard. Both were major kinks in my quest for a perfect childhood.

I thought about my magnificent Christmas list as I lay there in bed. It was at least a hundred miles long. I imagine

17

that if it had been dropped over the edge of the Empire State Building it would have stretched from top to bottom, then rolled into a manhole and landed in the abyss of the New York subway system. I could have easily just submitted the JCPenney catalog.

We always received our copy in the mail around Thanksgiving. I would find a spot on the floor and drag that paper monstrosity across my lap, using every tiny muscle in my body. With a crinkled nose reflecting my disgust, I would flip the pages past the bras and girdles to get to the toy section. Mr. Penney probably fired the person who was responsible for putting that most beloved section all the way in the back.

There were a few staples in every child's collection of toys. Although Slinkies were among the top, Crayola Crayons probably took the lead. I gripped my favorite blue one in my hand and circled all the toys that I deemed worthy to adorn my wish list. There were Nerf footballs and Hot Wheels cars, Star Wars action figures and Tomy Pocket Games. I wore that crayon down until I was peeling away the paper from around it. Then I reached the most coveted creation of plastic innovation ever imagined. Its picture glistened from among the outdoor toys, somewhere between the bicycles and trampolines. It was a navy blue and yellow Batman Bigwheel!

Nothing said cool like a Bigwheel. These plastic tricycles—with the pedals attached to the oversized front wheel—were built for speed. The adjustable seat sat between the back wheels just inches from the ground, giving its rider the look of pure street dominance. The caped-crusader colors and graphics only accentuated its greatness. There was no doubt that this speed machine would proudly grace the top of my list.

That Christmas was a bit different from the rest. My holiday break from school began early when tiny red spots started appearing all over my small white body. My view of chickens was never the same. Their annoying pox had disrupted my holiday plans. My mother had quarantined me in the house, and if Santa were to come through with the Bigwheel my chances of riding it looked slim. There was no way my mother was going to expose the world to that vile disease.

Being confined inside our house with the chicken pox wasn't too bad. Not only was I missing a few extra days of yucky arithmetic at school, but I also managed to catch most of the holiday television specials. Our Zenith tube TV had rabbit-ear antennae that reached into the sky, with aluminum foil crinkled around their tips for better reception. They looked more like a device used to communicate with aliens from distant planets. Through lines of static the TV illuminated the familiar images of *Frosty the Snowman, A Charlie Brown Christmas, Rudolph the Red-Nosed Reindeer,* and the greatest of them all: *How the Grinch Stole Christmas.* I never understood why Dr. Seuss wasted his time on being a doctor when he was so good at telling stories. I'm sure his inspiration for *Green Eggs and Ham* came from his own childhood sufferings with sauerkraut and weenies.

The night seemed to go on forever. Then, suddenly, there were noises coming from the hallway. *RIP! CLANK! TEAR! CLINK!* My ears bent from the sides of my head like panels on a satellite. *Could that be Santa Claus in my living room?* I crawled out from under the covers and slid along the shag carpet to my bedroom door. One squeak from my end and the whole operation would be thwarted. I had to be stealth. This was my chance to get a firsthand look at Kris Kringle, my chance to dispel all the rumors at school that the man in red didn't exist.

Gently I opened the door and peered out. There was movement in the living room at the other end. I heard the sounds of shuffling boxes, rattling paper, and clinking and clanking! My full-bodied footed pajamas were the perfect camouflage for the Delta Force Soldier I'd just become. I crawled slowly toward the light. Our short hallway seemed like a quadrillion miles long. My heart was beating outside my chest, and at one point I had to remove it and put it in my pocket to stop the pounding. This was it. One look around the corner and my prayers would be answered.

I was taking an enormous risk. Sure, I had done other stupid things in my short life that bordered insanity. You've read about the time when, as a kindergartener, I ran across the classroom like a wild animal during the pledge of allegiance. There was also the time I stole bubble gum from an open package at the dime store, only to be caught by my angry mother. She made me apologize to the manager and pay him the handful of pennies I had in my pocket. Crime doesn't pay, and neither did the preacher's wife. Being caught roaming around the house on Christmas night could be catastrophic. My curiosity seemed to outweigh my fear of certain death, and I inched closer to the living room.

I had reached the end. Visions of Saint Nick's fluffy white beard and bright red suit circled in my head as if they were angelic beings. I moved closer to the edge. *Had he already eaten the cookies and milk I had left for him?* I saw our glowing Christmas tree, some unassembled plastic wheels, piles of wrapping paper, and his shiny black boots extending into *blue jeans?* I shook my head in disbelief. Buck Owens and his Buckaroos were right when they sang: *Santa Looked A Lot Like Daddy!*

With a dash and a flash of lightning, I slipped back into the shadows unnoticed. I couldn't believe what I had seen. My feet began to sweat as I shuffled them back and forth to my bedroom. I gently closed the door and jumped back into bed. Part of me went into utter shock, but then I remembered those wheels. A smile appeared again and my eyes slowly shut.

No one really knows the moment in time when a child finally falls asleep the night before Christmas, but somehow it miraculously happens. The house falls silent with only the sounds of crickets chirping in the wilderness outside, and of the imagined hoots of a night owl. The clock ticked on.

The next morning, the sun rose bigger and brighter than usual. Our neighborhood witnessed a polka-dotted kid, dressed in a dark cape, white helmet, and footed pajamas, cruising down the street on his navy-blue and yellow Batman Bigwheel.

It Was That Dang Red-Headed Preacher's Kid!

"Holy sleeping bag, Batman!"

It Was That Dang Red-Headed Preacher's Kid!

THE PREACHER

Unwanted. That is how my life began on this earth. My biological mother, for whatever reason, decided that she wasn't ready to have a child, so she placed me for adoption. She gave birth to me in a Dallas hospital and then walked out the door when she could. I never knew her. Fortunately, the preacher and his wife adopted me, and I left with them through a different door. The scenario could have been a platform for disaster. I could have grown up with strong feelings of rejection, bitterness, and hurt, somehow feeling at fault for a circumstance beyond my control. My new parents raised me in a loving home, so I have never looked back. I have never felt as if I belonged to someone else.

For me, the beauty of adoption is that while I was once looked upon as a burden, I became someone specifically chosen with intentionality. Great costs have been paid and enormous sacrifices made so that I could be given a second chance. To be adopted is to be given a glimpse of hope. Adoption is a powerful act of love where a child can receive the full heritage of the embracing parents. My parents were able to adopt me because of their own humble beginnings in loving homes.

*   *   *   *

Life was simple in the 1950s, especially in the small rural community of Burnet, Texas. The town nestled in the hill country northwest of Austin was home to a minute population of farmers, local businessmen, and road construction workers. Those folks believed in hard work and strong family values. The surrounding countryside was acres of aging oak and cedar trees on beds of granite rock and limestone, colored with magnificent Indian paintbrushes and bluebonnets in sprinkles of red and purple.

The preacher was born into an age of innovation and a generation of hard workers. The expanding automobile industry was producing vehicles that would later define an era—long, broad-bodied cars with signature pointed tail fins, big engines, and glistening chrome bumpers and trim. But it was the mechanics under the hood that fascinated this curious, eleven-year-old boy, and my father wasn't afraid to disassemble a carburetor and get his hands greasy. In fact, he spent most of his weekends digging through my grandfather's toolbox, and tinkering with dysfunctional gadgets around the house that needed repair.

Every Saturday was an especially welcomed day because it rescued him from a boring, never-ending week of school, which was a constant struggle for him academically. It tested his patience. He would much rather breathe the strong fumes from the exhaust of a filthy muffler than have his nose stuck in the dreadful pages of an English textbook. Every Sunday was an important day of the week too when his family would faithfully attend the local Baptist church. Among the tall-suited deacons and well-dressed ladies with their towering, lacy hats, was this chubby, narrow-eyed, dark-headed boy sitting in between his older siblings on the long, wooden pews. My father was nicely dressed, except for a few wrinkles in his collared shirt, and his well-combed hair was slick and neatly parted to one side.

The congregation joined in singing a few hymns, following along in the hymnals held in one hand while fervently waving the church bulletin in the other to ease the summer heat. Next, they were all seated as the pastor positioned himself at the pulpit to deliver his sermon while the fanning continued. There were a few coughs and "amens," and somewhere during the preaching, the boy's attention drifted. His eyes moved from his fidgeting hands to the tiles on the ceiling. No one knew what was working in his mind, what he was thinking about as he carefully counted each tile above him. He counted them all: 2,346 total. The corner of his mouth lifted slightly with a feeling of success. Then he took a half chewed, dull pencil out of the pocket of his pants and opened his small Gideon New Testament Bible. On the inside cover, between other doodling and sketches, he recorded the number of tiles he had counted as if discovering a revolutionary mathematical equation. His imagination was like every other kid—wild, carefree, and reckless. But my father was different than the others because his heart dreamed of fixing things and making them better. What the boy didn't know was that one day he would fix things that had an eternal significance.

The years went by, and my father grew into a bright young man. He completed more years in high school than most of his peers but eventually graduated and moved on, in search of a destiny that had marked him for greatness. He was hired on as an electrician for a local company and found himself stringing wires, installing lights, and testing plugs at another Baptist Church. It was no coincidence, because it was during this time that he met the love of his life, my mother. She had an infectious smile and a beehive hairdo that was taller than basketball legend Earvin "Magic" Johnson. It was

27

swirly too, like twisted chocolate and vanilla ice cream in a cone. The two were soon married.

Something happens to a man when he discovers his passion. A sense of purpose is born and the need to satisfy this craving brings him to a defining moment; the place where he embraces his calling. My father set off on a new path, one that strengthened his character and expanded his horizons. The next few years would prepare him for his mission, taking him through change, adversity, and risk. He worked hard as a Volkswagen mechanic, digging through his Snap-on toolbox and changing carburetors to pay the bills. He attended seminary and studied the Bible, knowing that he would soon stand in own church, not just to install a breaker box, but also to preach and repair broken lives.

That day finally came. Every Sunday morning, my father could be found standing in the doorway of the church, shaking hands and giving hugs, as the members left the sanctuary to go home to pot roast and peach cobbler. He was a man of vision, whose spirit was contagious and ideals absolute. His congregation knew him as a minister with integrity and a man of great influence. Behind his suit and tie was a genuine friend, and his loving wife, my mom, was a reflection of the same.

*　　　*　　　*　　　*

The family grew with my adoption, and my parents quickly discovered that my diapers had to be changed more frequently than the oil in their VW Beetle. The oil change might have been less messy. The year was 1971, and it was an important one in American history. Cigarette ads were banned from television in January, and the Golden Gate

Bridge's lights went out for an entire night from a power failure in December. In October, the Dallas Cowboys defeated the Patriots, 44-21, in the grand opening of Texas Stadium. The year also gave us Walt Disney World, Starbucks, *Dirty Harry*, the game Uno, Hard Rock Café, the first pocket calculator from Texas Instruments, actor Sean Astin, who starred in *The Goonies*, one of the best movies ever, and The Willy Wonka Candy Company. Who doesn't love Fun Dip, Nerds, and Bottle Caps candies?

The times I spent hanging out with my dad when I was growing up would leave a lasting impression on me. When he was busy sawing and hammering things out of scrap lumber in the shop, I was watching him from between the dusty cardboard boxes I had made into a secret hideout. When he was under the hood of a broken-down car, I was sitting on the garage rooftop behind him and watching down below. And when he was tucked away in his church office nose-deep in the Old Testament between Noah's ark and Goliath the giant Philistine, I was watching him as I passed his doorway, sliding down the slippery hallways in my socks. I was even watching what he was watching as we sat together in front of the television set in the family living room.

It Was That Dang Red-Headed Preacher's Kid!

My favorite photo of dad

It Was That Dang Red-Headed Preacher's Kid!

Jim Ed Hardaway

PRISON ESCAPES, SINKING SHIPS, AND
HIDING PLACES

The doorknob rattled and swung open as my dad came home from a full day at the church office. He was the pastor of our local Baptist church. Normal days for Dad meant working on Sunday's bulletin, meeting with deacons here and there regarding the dwindling budget, scribbling scriptures in his sermon notes, or reserving the community dunking booth for summer outreaches. And hardly a day went by that Dad didn't have to run into town for hospital visits. These visits were as important to a Baptist minister's daily routine as Welch's Grape Juice was to communion. I hated going to the hospital for visits. There was always a chance some vile germ would jump onto my arm, or I'd catch a painful glimpse of some elderly person's rump exposed out the backside of one of those revealing patient gowns!

Soon after he got home, evening shadows crept in around our small, wood-framed house as the sun slowly dropped below the horizon. On the outside of our home, a soft, blue light flickered through our front window, streaming from our television set in the living room. The vinyl cushions squeaked as Dad settled into the couch and grabbed the remote control. We called it the "clicker"—I guess because it made clicking noises when you pressed the buttons. The only thing greater than the invention of the clicker was second-run syndication, or reruns. That's when smaller TV networks acquired rights to air movies and

33

television shows over and over and over. I'd drag handfuls of Star Wars action figures and playsets into the living room and bury myself in the shag carpet to watch TV with dad.

Dad was a master channel surfer. That's someone who clicks through every available channel on the television multiple times. Now, there are many reasons a man loves to channel surf. First, it's simply to aggravate the mom, who eventually wanders off into the other room mumbling things under her breath. Another reason a man channel surfs is to watch several shows at once ... in a determined dance to avoid the lame commercials. Some of my dad's favorite shows to land on were *M*A*S*H*, *The Rockford Files*, *Quincy*, and *Trapper John, M.D.* I remember that show because one of the doctors named *Gonzo,* like the Muppet, lived in a motor home in the hospital parking lot!

Dad's TV shows occasionally kept my attention, but most of the time I was busy chasing TIE Fighters with X-wing Fighters through the galaxy. The coffee table made a great Rebel base; that was until *click*, *click*, *click*, and dad channel surfed right into a thriller movie. I loved movies! There were a couple of movies that dad loved too and, thanks to reruns, he'd stop and watch them every time. There was no manly way possible to channel surf past them! I'd crash-land my star fighters and glue myself to the TV screen too; the Rebel base would have to defend itself for the next two hours.

Some of the best movies were about prison escapes, sinking ships, and hiding places. The first was about the most notorious prison of all time; it was called *Escape From Alcatraz.* Superstar Clint Eastwood was in it! I sat so close to that TV set that my head was tilted back, my jaw dropped, and my red bowl-cut hair glowed a subtle shade of purple.

Most of the movie was dark and spooky, with lots of lightning flashes, creepy prison cells, and mean-looking prisoners all wearing matching clothes. Except for this one guy, he had a big nose and his name was Charley Butts! That made me laugh—*Butts!* My mom didn't like that word and somehow heard it from the other room. I think she had bionic ears like Colonel Steve Austin from the television show *The Six Million Dollar Man*. Remind me to tell you about the time I said the word *crap!* It was a miracle I saw my 13th birthday.

The worst scene in *Escape from Alcatraz* happened in the wood shop. An old prisoner named *Doc* chopped his fingers off with a hatchet because the warden took away his painting privileges. Good thing I still had my own fingers to cover my eyes because that was freaky! Charley Butts got wobbly kneed too and almost passed out! Every second of that movie was thrilling as we cheered for Mr. Eastwood and his buddies to break out of The Rock—secret tunnels, scary paper-mache' heads, and lots of Bible reading. That's why Dad liked it.

Another movie we loved to watch was *The Poseidon Adventure* starring Gene Hackman, when he was younger and had more hair. He was a reverend in the movie, *Reverend Scott*, and I started to see why Dad liked these movies. Unlike my dad, Reverend Scott yelled at God a lot and said dirty words. I think it was because he paid too much for his cruise ticket and then the ship flipped. You see, that's what happened in the movie. A ginormous tidal wave flipped the ship over during a New Year's party, and a group of survivors had to escape before it sank. Everything was upside-down! I imagined the movie makers had to stand on their heads just to build the extravagant sets. There were explosions and flash fires, lots of rushing water and girls screaming, and even a big blue Christmas tree!

I grew up with revivals, churchwide picnics, dunking booths, campfires, potluck dinners, baptisms, late-night prayer meetings, and yes, even a few of those notorious deacons meetings along the way. There were breakdowns on church buses, holes in baptismal waders, thousands of plastic Lord's Supper cups filled, snakes in choir rooms, inadequate budgets, and offering plates passed twice. On bad days, there were toilets that overflowed and grumpy old ladies that complained about the music, but there were also good days when everyone showed up for the annual Sunday night showing of the movie *The Hiding Place*. Yes, we even had movie night at the house of God!

For movie night, the preacher pulled out the church's dusty movie projector from the closet underneath the baptistry. The room was dark except for a ray of light streaming from that reel-to-reel projector. The audience was quiet and still as the film tape spun across the reels and the electric motor made a clicking sound as it pulled the footage across the front of the bulb. Dust particles swirled around in the flickering light like tiny mystical fairies, dancing to the current of the air circulating in the small sanctuary. I sat slumped on the hardwood pew, clinching the edge of my Sears Rustlers corduroy pants with each hand, my legs dangling over the edge, too short to reach the floor. I was mesmerized by the stirring images illuminating the screen and the emotional story they told.

The Hiding Place is the true story of Casper ten Boom, an elderly watchmaker, and his two daughters, Corrie and Elizabeth, or Betsie. The year was 1940, and they lived in Haarlem, Holland when the Nazis invaded, during the darkest days of World War II. The Ten Booms' charitable hearts kept them active in the city's Dutch underground, where they secretively helped hide Jewish refugees from Adolf Hitler's murderous regime. They managed to harbor a handful of Jews in a hidden closet known as *the hiding place.* My eyeballs stared intently at those characters and images flashing out the story on the large projector screen.

A bitter February day in 1944 delivered a devastating blow to their humanitarian service. Thanks to a cold tip from a Dutch informant, the Ten Booms were found out and arrested by angry Gestapo agents. Old man Casper died in prison just 10 days after their capture, and Corrie and Betsie were sent to a political camp in the Netherlands. In September, they were both sent to the notorious Ravensbrück concentration camp near Berlin, Germany, where they were exposed to disease, malnourishment, unimaginable filthy conditions, hateful abuse, and lice. The cooties part grossed me out, and my hair mysteriously started itching!

Betsie eventually died at the concentration camp. Despite these horrendous conditions — but not without doubt and fear of uncertainty — Corrie kept her faith in God. She was released on December 30, 1944, at age 53. She later learned her release happened because of a clerical error.

Watching movies like these and playing with LEGO bricks and Tinkertoy construction sets always fueled my imagination. My mom did too. She sewed me a Batman cape from an old navy blue sheet to tie around my neck, so I could fight crime in Gotham City. I even carried around an old golf club as my Jedi lightsaber, watching out for Darth Vader, who was lurking in the shadows to spy on my tree house. Other times, I carried around a piece of rope like Indiana

Jones, trying to crack it against the skulls of make-believe scoundrels attempting to steal my treasure map. Those were the good 'ol days when my love for movies and adventure was born, and it was only the beginning.

Shaving like the preacher

It Was That Dang Red-Headed Preacher's Kid!

PLAYGROUND SUPERHEROES

The bell rang—*KKKKLLLLAAAANNNNGGGG!* Kids flew in every direction as Mrs. S, our grumpy old school teacher, barked at us to form a single-file line next to the classroom door. Mrs. S had curly, gray hair with white streaks in it and wore cat-eye glasses. She was rather plump too. Mrs. S gripped a wooden ruler in her hand and waved it around in the air like Darth Vader with his lightsaber. We dodged that ruler's fiery furry like Jedi Knights and hurriedly scrambled into place as if our lives depended on it. It was almost impossible for second graders to stand still, knowing that we only had 35 minutes of recess ahead of us. We couldn't contain our hyperactivity.

Most of the children in our small-town elementary school had been diagnosed with hyperactivity. The teachers said we were infested with it, especially the boys. Adults had the daunting task of determining if kids couldn't stand still because they were hyper, or just had to go to the bathroom. Jumping to the wrong conclusion could be disastrous!

My hyperactivity caused me to dance uncontrollably in my Toughskin jeans with the reinforced knees. Moms dressed their kids in these jeans from Sears because they were rugged and cheap. My mother dressed me in Toughskin jeans because they were practically indestructible and came in all sorts of cool colors like denim blue and magenta. Toughskins were required active wear for kids who played outside from sunup to sundown. I wore Toughskin jeans inside the house, outside the house, to play, to school, to church, to McDonald's for Happy Meals, to Vacation Bible School, on campouts, and I would have slept in them if I could have gotten away with it.

Mrs. S, after corralling us for 5 minutes, finally gave in and led us down the long, noisy hallway and out the side door of the school building to our beautiful, gravel-covered playground. Once we cleared the threshold, it was a mad sprint to claim one of the highly coveted seesaws, swings, or a place on the multi-colored, nauseating merry-go-round. Not my friend Matthew and I. We had our eyes fixed on the twisted web of gray steel that rose high into the sky like a cloud-splitting skyscraper and formed the greatest set of glorious monkey bars the world has ever seen!

I was Batman and Matthew was Robin, at least in our vivid childhood imaginations. The monkey bars were our Batcave, and Monday through Friday, it was our crime-fighting duty to protect our cave against the evil villains who were out to expose its hidden secrets. Our friend Rodges was our archenemy, the Joker. He and his mischievous gang of criminals came at us from every direction. Matthew and I would swing down from the top of the monkey bars, using our Batropes, and the fight was on. *BAM!* I raised my arm to block a swing from The Joker. *POW!* Matthew countered with a punch to his evil sidekick. *BOOM!* The Joker sent me to the dirt with a last-minute trip.

Every once in a while a stinky girl would appear from nowhere to join the action. That meant all the seesaws and swings were taken and she wanted to climb the Batcave. Knowing we would get in trouble if she squealed on us for not letting her play, we would quickly call her "Batgirl" and let her on the monkey bars. *YUCK!*

Thirty-five minutes seemed more like only 10, and before we knew it, the bell rang to announce recess was over— *KKKKLLLLAAANNNNGGGG!* The playground superheroes were done for the day. Matthew and I dusted off our Toughskin jeans and jeered at the villains to let them know we'd be back the next day. The Joker always leaped on the Batcave as if he'd won the brawl, but we knew better. The good guys always win in the end and save the day. We growled and snarled at each other as we walked back to the school to get in line. *SWOOSH!* We all dodged as Mrs. S swung her monstrous wooden ruler. *WACK!*

It Was That Dang Red-Headed Preacher's Kid!

It's almost time for recess!

It Was That Dang Red-Headed Preacher's Kid!

Jim Ed Hardaway

THE SCRAWNY LITTLE LEAGUER

I ran as fast as I could. My stiff blue jeans made a brushing sound as my legs passed each other going back and forth in a full sprint. The neighborhood dogs barked in a frenzy and chased me as I ran down the sidewalk beside a long chain-link fence. The untied laces of my sneakers flapped like the ears on a basset hound, and the worn-out soles kicked up dust as I made a swift turn on to our driveway toward the front door. It was my first time ever to play Little League Baseball. Waiting for me inside the house was the news of what team I would play on.

The screen door slammed closed behind me as I dashed into the house. There it was, calling to me from across the room. The sounds of an angelic choir sang in my imagination as I stared in awe at its beaming glow. The late-afternoon sunlight streamed through the window and illuminated that coveted baseball uniform like a lightning bug at a campout. It was neatly laid on the dining room table; it had creases and folds that only a mother could make. There was a bright-red baseball cap with a bold white C crested above the bill. Beside it, with the same crimson glow, were a T-shirt that read *Cardinals* across the front and a pair of white baseball pants.

There was no time to waste; I had to try it on. I pulled that oversized T-shirt over my bowl-cut hair and tucked it so deep into the white polyester pants that you could barely read the team name. Those elastic waist pants pulled up to just below my chest. I was a scrawny 10-year-old kid, one of

47

the smallest on the team, and my big ears stuck out the sides of that cap like the wings on the Space Shuttle. The uniform was way too big, but that didn't matter.

One day, my parents drove me to the practice field next to the red-bricked middle school. I dreaded every mile as our car sped over the battered asphalt, because there was an older kid on the team who had been bullying all the younger players. My nemesis was a portly kid named Scott, and I was scared to death of him. Scott had more freckles scattered across his paunchy face than cupcakes have sprinkles, and a piercing, cold stare that burned a hole through your skin. He gave me the heebie-jeebies so much so that my bony kneecaps shook violently, as we got closer to the field.

My parents dropped me off behind the rickety old backstop behind home plate, and my pitiful shoulders sagged as I stood there in my dusty cleats and watched them drive away. In the next few minutes, I prayed and promised God that I would keep my pigsty of a bedroom clean forever if He would please let one of the coaches arrive before Scott did; that was the only way I would be safe from his devilish menace. It didn't happen. I saw Scott coming toward me across the field, his eyes already burning a hole through my delicate flesh, and a look of disgust spread across his face like he'd just gargled nails and been released from prison. I was shaking in my undersized cleats as I tossed my baseball into the air in an effort to ignore him. That didn't work either. I was clearly locked into his radar and in line to be his next unfortunate victim.

Scott walked straight up to me and bumped me with his well-upholstered chest, then leaned his sun-scorched face next to my ear. His words mixed with his reeking breath as he told me he was going to take off my pants, hang them in

48

the tree, and leave me stranded in my tighty-whitey underwear for all to see. I was absolutely mortified! The scene ran through my head like a nightmare, and I was completely defenseless. If only I had a baseball bat in my hand instead of that stupid glove, I might have stood a chance. So, I did the only thing I could—I ran. *SWOOSH!* This action was totally appropriate considering the fact that I was terrified at the mere thought of my own indecent exposure.

I had no idea where I was going, but I ran as fast as my skinny body could go, leaving my synthetic leather glove as collateral and my baseball cap sailing off into the wind. Scott was hot on my heels! There was a neighborhood on the other side of the tree line—behind the field—and I *had* to make it to one of the houses. I wheezed with every stride, and my throat burned from the humid air, but there was no way I was going to slow down. I had a few things working to my advantage: my speed, my love for Cap'n Crunch cereal, and a fear for my life. Finally, he gave up the chase letting me fade away into the distance. I could hear his mockery and laughter echoing behind me as I disappeared into the trees. I can still hear it today.

It Was That Dang Red-Headed Preacher's Kid!

Jim Ed Hardaway

Up your nose with a rubber hose, Scott!

51

It Was That Dang Red-Headed Preacher's Kid!

LEMONADE MOONSHINE

I grew up in small-town America where long lines of traffic piled up behind tractors occupying a single-lane highway. Towns where everybody went to the local high-school football game on Friday night just because it was Texas State law. Towns where the local donut shop was filled with old men on Saturday mornings—men griping about politicians and reminiscing about the Vietnam War. On that same Saturday morning kids would flock into Milt's Mini Mart—with pockets full of quarters—to spend them all in the only Pac Man arcade machine for miles. Towns where occasionally a bale of hay would fall off the back of a beat-up old pickup truck traveling on a dirt road. They were winding, dusty roads beneath giant pecan trees, lined with barbed wire fences on either side and grazing cattle in the distant fields. I rode my bicycle down many of those roads, pretending I was Bo Duke in the General Lee, being chased by Sheriff Rosco P. Coltrane in hot pursuit.

I was obsessed with the Good Ol' Boys—The Dukes! As far as I was concerned, our county was Hazzard County, and I had a distant make-believe relative named Uncle Jesse and a smokin' hot cousin named Daisy, whom I could *not* marry some day because it would make things complicated. This was an upsetting situation I tried working out in my fifth-grade mind on many occasions because, although I was from the South, I did not go to the family reunion to look for women.

God bless CBS for airing *The Dukes of Hazzard,* one of the greatest action-packed shows in television history! Not only was it one of my favorite TV shows for its highly anticipated adventures, but it had one of the coolest cars in it since Adam West and Burt Ward's jet-black Batmobile! Bo and Luke Duke blazed around Hazzard County in a 1969 Dodge Charger. I can still see the flashing light of the television screen as that Hemi Orange muscle car—with the number "01" on the doors—slid around dangerous curves and jumped high in the air over rocky riverbeds. It belted out its signature horn, which played the melodic sounds of "Dixie." I could never convince my father to install one of those horns on the handlebars of my bike.

Those high-speed stunts and chases were spectacular, but why would a couple of good ol' boys be running from the law? Well, the Duke brothers had a past history of running illegal moonshine, and their hillbilly Uncle Jesse had a habit of brewing it. This put the Dukes on the bad side of the devious and scheming, cigar-totin' Jefferson Davis "Boss" Hogg, Hazzard County's corrupt commissioner.

I remember going to visit my grandparents in the hill country and playing *The Dukes of Hazzard* with my friend Johnny, who lived down the road. His older brothers hid their nasty girly magazines under an old blanket in the corner of his tree house. I was Bo Duke, Johnny was Luke Duke, and my granny would make us a tall pitcher of cold lemonade to use as our moonshine. We would run around her yard, sweating in the summer heat and sipping on plastic cups of our refreshing "lemonade moonshine." We kept a sharp eye out for Boss Hogg and Rosco P. Coltrane. I would drive the General Lee while Johnny would shoot his bow and dynamite-laced arrows at the law. Every once in a while we'd find some random kids to play Rosco, Deputy Enos, or Cooter the mechanic. Nobody ever wanted to be Boss Hogg — *"Get them Duke Boys!"* Our attractive cousin Daisy Duke accompanied us only in our imaginations, because we didn't want a real-life stinky girl ruining the part. Sometimes Pa Pa's shed out back doubled as the Boar's Nest, a local restaurant and bar where Daisy worked.

Don't ask me how a Southern Baptist preacher's kid got away with drinking "moonshine," getting in trouble with the law, and fantasizing about a scantily dressed brunette in her signature high-cut Daisy Duke short shorts! Ahh, but those were the good ol' days as we pretended to be the good ol' boys. And I can still sing every word to the theme song sung by country singer Waylon Jennings.

It Was That Dang Red-Headed Preacher's Kid!

Rosco P. Coltrane is in hot pursuit!

It Was That Dang Red-Headed Preacher's Kid!

A LAKE, SOME CREEKS, AND THAT LEECH-INFESTED SWAMP!

It was hotter than h-e-double-hockey-sticks growing up in South Texas. My Aunt Carolyn would've washed my mouth out with soap for saying "hell," a surefire remedy for curing even the mildest of profanities. It was true nonetheless. There were only two seasons in Texas during the year; summer lasted for about 11 months, and a mixture of fall, winter, and spring made up the other month. It wasn't uncommon for me to be wearing a tank top and cut-off shorts at Christmastime. If we were lucky, we'd have a handful of days in the year when it was cold enough for me to wear a stocking cap and a coat, but my mom still smeared ungodly amounts of sunscreen all over me. As I said before, it only took 10 seconds of me being in the sun to get blistered! I sunburned so bad my mom had to keep me away from lightbulbs when I was indoors, and covered me from head-to-toe in sunscreen when I was outdoors.

Texans were in water from spring break until Thanksgiving to avoid a heatstroke. I spent most of my childhood playing in some form of water. If I wasn't splashing around in a lake, creek, or pond, I was riding my bicycle to get from one to the other. When I was a teenager and got my drivers license, I went to the beach. It was pretty simple really: eat and swim. If there was any extra time in a day I would sleep and dream about swimming. Yep, I have a lot of memories of certain bodies of water, from going to family reunions on the lake, to diving for shiny coins in my Aunt Brenda's backyard swimming pool, to wearing my bright-orange arm floaties and jumping off the high dive at the public pool. Floaties were inflatable armbands you'd wear on your arms to keep from drowning, and boy did I love 'em! I never took those glorious water wings off and my mother would have to wrestle them away to get me in the bathtub.

When I was growing up, we spent every summer at my grandparents' house in the hill country near Austin. We'd load up the lawn chairs, inner tubes, and ice chests early in the morning; jump in the back of pickup trucks; and take off on what seemed to be a forever drive to a watering hole called *Cow Creek*. It doesn't take much beyond grub and a place to dip your feet to entertain a group of Texans. Cow Creek had it all: running streams, trickling rapids, and best of all a waterfall! Why does everything seem ginormous when you're a kid? I remember standing mortified at the top of that waterfall—my knees shaking—while my dad waited in the deep waters below waving for me to jump. Life was too precious! I would find out later the waterfall was only about four feet tall.

Another popular hill-country destination was Inks Lake State Park. We'd have our annual family reunion there with horseshoe and fishing tournaments and everything! It was hard to beat the old folks at horseshoes, and it was a miracle if somebody caught anything bigger than a six-inch perch when fishing. Uncle Bob would bring trophies for the winner of each. And speaking of Uncle Bob, nobody on the planet blew their nose like him! There were arm-wrestling competitions, hot-dog-eating competitions, even office-chair-racing competitions. If there ever were a nose-blowing match, my Uncle Bob would leave all competitors crying next to their Kleenex boxes. His nose blowing was quite a feat and something our family was very proud of.

Uncle Bob is to nose-blowing what Louis Armstrong is to trumpets, or even Gabriel the archangel for that matter. When Gabriel goes to blast his great trumpet in the clouds, when the saints go marching in, he had better hope it's not allergy season, because Uncle Bob will give him a run for his money! It is quite possible that the angel might be looking for a new job.

My two favorite things at Inks Lake were the country store at the cove and Camp Longhorn. The Mrs. Baird's cherry pies from the store would hit the spot when I was starving from swimming all day, and I got to see teenage girls in bikinis if we drove the boat close enough when passing by the camp! It was fun being a kid at the lake—that was until my cousins told me the story about the boat that went over the side of the dam and killed all its passengers. I threatened to jump overboard in my floaties if they ever drove our boat too close to that dam, and they seemed to get a kick out of seeing me squirm when they did so! Years later, I learned how to waterski and waved at those pretty girls at the camp as I zoomed by.

When my dad became pastor at the Baptist church in the country, we moved into the parsonage behind the church next to Caney Creek. That's when the real adventures began. I built tunnels in the thick brush, navigated the currents in our flat-bottom boat, shot my .22 rifle at snakes and alligator gars in the water, and rode my Kawasaki dirt bike up and down the steep banks until it was out of gas. On my 14th birthday, my friends Korey, Bill, Mike, and I made a long mudslide that zig-zagged down the main trail to the creek bank. We were completely caked in mud, and it was still leaking out my ears weeks later.

If I wasn't exploring Caney Creek, I was hanging out at my best friend's—Dennis's—house. We spent a lot of time together, carving Star Wars spaceships out of Styrofoam, annoying his sister Virginia, and listening to 80s albums on his record player. Dennis's mom worked at Texas State Optical, an eyeglasses store in town, and she would sometimes take us to work with her during the summer. There was a movie theater next door, and we would watch movies back-to-back until she got off work. I think we watched *E.T. the Extra-Terrestrial* four times in a row one day!

Dennis too was adventurous, and we spent most of our time outdoors. His family had a duck pen in the backyard, and sometimes we'd spray the poo off the concrete pond with a water hose and then swim in it. There was also a small swamp in the cow pasture behind his house; it had a lot of moss in it and was kind of stinky. I remember one time Dennis caught a fish out of the swamp, and its gills were covered with tiny leeches—*leeches!* But that didn't stop us from putting on our goggles and snorkeling around through that murky water to look for treasures. Which reminds me, I never went to the doctor to get checked for leeches.

Cow Creek

It Was That Dang Red-Headed Preacher's Kid!

Jim Ed Hardaway

TALE OF THE SNIPE HUNTERS

We were surrounded by darkness, two friends alone and frozen with fear. Above us the midnight sky was as black as a cup of day-old coffee. The woods encircled us like prison walls and its trees stood like ominous guardians of the night. The thick air was humid, causing beads of sweat to build on our foreheads. It ran down our temples and spilled over our cheeks. Each drop that fell from our faces spattered on our forearms, causing a chain reaction of quivers and chills.

It was dark.

We sat crouched and motionless in the middle of an itchy hay field, each gripping the corner of a burlap potato sack with clinched fist. Dennis's father, Mr. H, had led us there earlier for an infamous Snipe hunt. Unlike a wild goose chase, Snipe hunting requires the hunter to be both stealth and patient, very patient.

Mr. H was a real adventurer and had taken us on exciting excursions before. We went on camping trips into the deep woods, and historical excavations on rivers and creek beds. He was a master storyteller and could easily captivate our attention with tales of everything from haunted houses to thrilling legends. I had plastic bags in my bedroom full of real Indian pottery and arrowheads we had dug up on many of our expeditions.

All Dennis and I had been told were that Snipes migrated to the region only once every several years, and we had a rare opportunity to catch some. This was bigger than a solar eclipse! The trick was to be absolutely still and to make some ridiculous whistling noise, which we did over-and-over-and-over again. *SHHWWEEEETT! SHHWWEEEETT! CLICK! CLICK! CLICK! SHHWWEEEETT! SHHWWEEEETT! SHHWWEEEETT! CLICK! CLICK! SHHWWEEEETT!* I can still hear that ridiculous sound echoing in my head. We watched and waited for the mysterious and deceptive birds, still frightened by the potential threats that could be preying on us from the woods.

We knew nothing about these strange Snipes, with nothing to go on but our wild imaginations. And if what I imagined was true, then we had more to be afraid of than the enveloping darkness. Cold shivers shook my softening spine like meatballs plopping on a bowl of spaghetti noodles. The very idea that these devil birds were watching us from the shadows made my knees weak.

The Snipe's oily burgundy feathers were stiffer than the fur on a wildebeest, so tough that they could slice through the quills of a porcupine. Rising from the crown of their heads were a pair of pointed horns, and their tail feathers split down the middle like a pitchfork. This gave the creature more agility and speed when alluding larger prey, or attacking unsuspecting hunters like us.

Their short, stubby wings were more for fluttering than flight, and hung rather clumsily on each side of their bodies. They gripped the earth with two large talons. The left one had four claws and the right had five! It was a disturbing oddity that could only be surpassed by its hideous beak. This small, pointed bill was lined with rows of jagged teeth.

Our eyes played tricks on us with façades of feathered creatures hopping around in the distance. We waited.

And waited.

And waited.

And watched.

And waited.

And whistled. *SHHWWWEEEETT! SHHWWWEEEETT! CLICK! CLICK! CLICK! SHHWWWEEEETT!*

And waited.

And watched.

And waited.

And watched.

And whistled some more. *SHHWWWEEEETT! CLICK! CLICK! SHHWWWEEEETT!*

And watched.

And waited.

Dennis and I whistled and watched and waited in that awful hay field for almost three hours, until we lost all hope of seeing any Snipes, much less catching one. It was almost two o'clock in the morning, and the sinister shadows were too much for us to bear. We were frightened to the core of our tiny bones. Finally we gave up and ran back to the campsite both tired and defeated.

The yellow and orange flames from the campfire danced in the distance, and grew larger as we got closer — its flicker made us run faster and its radiant glow lit up the faces of our fellow campers hovering around it for warmth. The smell of smoke filled our noses as we gasp for air from the long hustled sprint back from the woods. Our friends greeted us with hoots and applause and wails of laughter. Mr. H just grinned and didn't say a word.

That long and miserable night I learned that eating too many delicious s'mores would leave your stomach twisted into tangled knots. Crusty bits of marshmallow were still stuck to the peach fuzz on my upper lip. I learned to stay armed with a flashlight at all times when telling ghost stories, because ghosts are afraid of light. I also learned what it meant to be duped on a fool's errand, and that the illusive Snipe would forever evade the grasp of the human hand.

Then suddenly, we all froze! You could hear it in the distance over the smoldering wood crackling in our campfire. What was that fluttering sound in the darkness? *SHHWWWEEEETT! CLICK! CLICK! SHHWWWEEEETT!*

Snipe hunters

It Was That Dang Red-Headed Preacher's Kid!

THAT GALAXY FAR, FAR AWAY...

There was a small movie theater just off the downtown square of the town I grew up near. The Texas Theater had one of those iconic red-bordered marquees extending out over the sidewalk, with the brightly lit background and the lightbulbs around the edges that flashed to a mysterious beat. Stretched out across the middle on either side were those big, black, plastic letters that spelled out the name of the featured film. I remember my parents parking the car near the curb in 1977 and walking me across the street towards the ticket booth between the two front doors. "STAR WARS" gleamed from that magnificent sign over the gathering crowd below. I had no idea that I was about to see the greatest movie of all time.

Once inside, we dusted off the popcorn remnants from our seat cushions. Moments later, the house lights dimmed, and the audience fell silent, except for the ruffling of candy boxes and sporadic whispers. A beam of light streamed across the dark room from the noisy projector behind us. Blue words spread across the big screen that said: "A long time ago in a galaxy far, far away ..." Then suddenly a crescendo of intense music filled the speakers and launched us into the epic space story at light speed!

The screen flickered the most amazing sights I had ever seen. My eyeballs couldn't keep up with the mesmerizing spaceships, bleeping robots, and flashing lasers. And then, these white plastic-armored soldiers called *Stormtroopers* parted to make way for the greatest and most ominous villain in the history of bad guys: Darth Vader! He wore a strange helmet, an imposing black suit with the little red and green lights on his belt, and a long, flowing black cape. He had a terrifying asthma problem. I was entranced for the next two hours and didn't blink one time during the whole movie!

Star Wars had it all: comical droids, clashing futuristic swords called *lightsabers*, a hairy apelike creature named *Chewbacca*, strange planets, a ton of way cool spaceships like X-wings and TIE fighters, characters with weird last names like *Skywalker* and *Solo*, and a pretty princess with a hairdo I never thought possible on a woman. Princess Leia had side buns; she actually had brunette cinnamon rolls on both sides of her head!

I walked out of the theater that night with a ridiculous grin on my face and an unexplainable boost of energy that would last my entire childhood. The doors at the discount department store didn't open because they were automatic; they opened because I was a Jedi Knight and used the Force to move them with a simple wave of my hand, like Obi-Wan Kenobi could do. And speaking of department stores, I ran straight for the toy section of our local Kmart every time we went, to see what new *Star Wars* stuff had come out. A toy company called *Kenner* made starfighters, replica play sets, and action figures right from the movie. I'd load up armfuls of the stuff and then begin the exhausting search to find my mother so I could explain to her why it was necessary that I own them all. That never worked out the way I'd planned, but I would take home at least one new action figure. I remember one trip where I had saved my allowance and bought Luke Skywalker's landspeeder. A *landspeeder* was like a floating dune buggy with jet engines. That toy, and a few

72

action figures, made an appearance in my first home-movie taken with an 8mm camera.

Between my vast collection of *Star Wars* toys and my best friend Dennis's, we had everything. We'd spend all day together, reenacting scenes from the movie or making up new adventures. The sandbox in the old tractor tire behind his house was the desert planet Tatooine. Sometimes we'd blow up Stormtroopers with leftover firecrackers from the Fourth of July. We did have our share of galactic disagreements too. I always felt like Princess Leia belonged with Luke Skywalker, but Dennis argued that she was best with Han Solo. Boy, was he right! We found out later in the sequel *Return of the Jedi* that Leia was Luke's sister. I thought of all the times I had defiled those two action figures with a victory celebration kiss. *Gross!*

Dennis and I would eat, sleep, and drink all things *Star Wars*, including C-3PO cereal for breakfast! I would spend the night at his house, and we would carve out our own spaceships from Styrofoam with X-ACTO knives, or draw the entire Rebel Fleet in our spiral notebooks. One time we found some old golf clubs in the corner of my dad's garage. We cut off the heads of them and used them as lightsabers. They were way better than the inflatable toy ones from the store that would bend every time you swung them. Dennis and I would then run around the yard, dueling between trees until the day I wacked him in the shin with my golf-club-turned-lightsaber. I think that was the maddest I ever saw Dennis, and he chased me around for the next hour to seek revenge.

Our theater closed down a few years later and was taken over by the local charismatic church, as often happens in small-town America. We saw the *Star Wars* sequels *The*

Empire Strikes Back and *Return of the Jedi,* in the early 80s at newer theaters with bigger screens and surround sound. But the venue didn't matter to us. Somehow a man named George Lucas tapped into our imaginations and left the indelible mark of *Star Wars* on our brains forever. Call it creative genius or call it the *Force,* but it would be with us always.

Part-time motor home, part-time Imperial Star Destroyer!

It Was That Dang Red-Headed Preacher's Kid!

Jim Ed Hardaway

ALL I WANT FOR CHRISTMAS IS AN ATARI!

Christmas morning is a kid's most favorite morning of all the mornings in an entire year. The sun is still sneaking over from China; the roosters are still snug in their coops; and parents, for some odd reason, are still fast asleep. Until I became aware of the whole Santa conspiracy, I had no idea why parents insisted on sleeping in. The magic moment when a kid can get up on Christmas morning lies shrewdly and covertly between five-thirty and six o'clock in the morning. Deciding the precise minute it's safe to wake up the parents is completely at each child's own risk. I failed miserably more times than I had fingers, toes, and freckles to count. The anticipation for Christmas morning began with the traditional writing of my wish list to jolly 'ol Saint Nick.

There have been some extraordinary items on my Christmas lists over the years. My imagination peaked to pinnacle heights of momentous grandeur when it came to making a list of highly coveted toys, trinkets, and games to get from Santa Claus. I remember the "Chicken Pox Christmas" when I got that glorious Batman Big Wheel. I wore the tread off those plastic wheels before Saint Patty's Day. Also under our brilliantly colorful Christmas tree that year were the Dynamic Duo—Batman and Robin action figures! There was also a Joker action figure, because no crime fighting would be complete without an evil villain to conquer. That Christmas goes down in history as one of the most epic of all time.

Then there was the pigskin Christmas. My most favorite football team was the Dallas Cowboys, so Santa made sure that every square inch of my scrawny, pale body was covered in navy blue, silver, and white. I got Cowboys jackets, T-shirts, hats, and socks; even a training camp shirt with the number 33 from my favorite football player Tony Dorsett! There was no question that I had become the greatest fan the storied franchise had ever seen. But that wasn't all, I also got an Atomic Arcade Pinball machine and a handheld Entex LED Space Invader Arcade game. *Holy electronics, Batman!* I think my parents must have bought a gazillion batteries that year.

Those were some memorable holidays from my childhood, when forgetting to look both ways when you crossed the street was as common as forgetting to brush your teeth. When I became a teenager my Christmas lists progressed like my personal hygiene habits. I made sure to cake on thick layers of deodorant, and I drank Scope mouth wash like it was a soda. There were bigger things to dream about than 64-count boxes of crayons with the built-in sharpener on the box — things like BMX bikes, boogie boards, VHS tapes of my favorite movies, and enticing colognes. Thanks to Atari, Inc., video computer systems were on most Christmas lists, and holding the number one spot at the top of my list in the early 80s was their prized Atari 2600 video-game console.

The morning light broke through my bedroom window that Christmas morning, as I stretched and yawned and crawled out of bed. When you became a teenager you were still excited about Christmas mornings, but you managed a single ounce of self-control to stay in bed a tad longer. Puberty did strange things and you didn't want to

78

overshadow your obvious signs of maturity, like peach fuzz on your upper lip, by appearing too anxious. I shuffled my stinky bare feet down the hallway weaving my way passed the kitchen, zig-zagging through the dining area, and finally into our living room. There it sat beneath the Christmas tree, in its magnificent dazzling-colored box. An electronic ring of light glowed around it in a sunset tint of amber, and the melodic piano sounds of the Vince Guaraldi Trio played in the cosmos.

My parents quietly appeared in the background, a signal that it was now legal to tear open my gifts. The red and green bows on each present stared at me as if begging to be opened first, but they would all have to wait. I gently took that Atari 2600 box in my hands and pulled open one side. I slid out the Styrofoam protected contents to reveal the stunning game console with its elegant wood veneer, space-age silver control switches, and four black and orange joystick and paddle controllers. Also included were the game cartridges Pong and Combat, and I soon opened another present containing the popular Pacman. I adored that round, yellow, chomping character and his gobbling ghosts like I adored that most rad Christmas.

During the following months, my parents could find me stuck at the Atari video-game display in JC Penney's while shopping at the mall. I stood there for hours, staring—with my head tilted in wonderment—at the rows and rows of colorful game cartridges for the Atari 2600. My collection of games eventually grew to include Vanguard, Space Invaders, Astroids, Centipede, Missile Command, Pitfall, and the mysterious Yars' Revenge.

It Was That Dang Red-Headed Preacher's Kid!

Atari with mom

It Was That Dang Red-Headed Preacher's Kid!

Jim Ed Hardaway

HURRICANE GHOST STORY

Lightning cracked through the dark, stormy sky, illuminating the dense cumulonimbus clouds hovering above us. Heavy drops of rain and hail splattered on the windows as we nervously watched to see if the glass would crack. Our knees clanked together like the metal balls on Newton's cradle. We were sitting in a small room with big windows covering two walls, the windows giving the thunderstorm an advantage in the fear factor. Rolls of rumbling thunder followed every crack of lightning, creating a haunting orchestration of sounds that rattled the aging hardwood floors and echoed down the hallways. The glass in the windowpanes seemed to bow in with every roll of thunder.

A small gang of kids had gathered in the room, led there by my buddy Bill and me. We were the ringleaders, the two oldest in the bunch. At 12 years old we were just one year away from being official teenagers, so the other children looked up to us. And we definitely took advantage of the situation.

It was hurricane season in south Texas, and my father, the preacher, always opened up the church for members to take shelter if needed. Hurricane Alicia was knocking at our doors, and the weatherman predicted that the tropical cyclone would bring destruction. That prediction was enough to cause several families in the congregation to pack a few essentials, throw the kids in the station wagon, and gather in the church building.

All the parents and senior citizens sat in a long, narrow room behind the fellowship hall, playing cards and flipping dominoes. It looked and sounded like a Vegas casino in there, without the cigarette smoke and dirty words, of course. It was a family environment because all the deacons stayed at home to watch HBO. We kids took advantage of running around that ginormous old building in our socks, sliding around every corner in feverish games of hide-and-seek. That's how we ended up in that front room with all the windows.

It was a perfect time and place for ghost stories.

Ghost stories are an important part of a child's life. We told scary stories at campouts, at sleepovers, and on hayrides. It's what we did to keep our attention off the disgusting teenagers who were making out at the back of the trailer, underneath the hay where the youth pastor couldn't see them. Bill and I sat on two metal folding chairs in front of the other children, who sat facing us on the floor. Their backs faced those walls of windows and the horrendous storm outside.

No telling of ghost stories could be complete without the legend of the Hasema Wild Woman, a favorite in our small community. Hasema Road was a narrow, winding, dirt road that ran through the backwoods in our county. It had more potholes that anyone could count, which forced people to drive slow as they moved along. The trees stood tall on either side, casting shadows on the road and looking like skeletons. The woods were so thick that they eclipsed the sunlight, making it scary even in the daytime. The road went on for miles into the woods, and at the halfway point were an old, abandoned church and a cemetery.

Bill and I spoke in our scariest voices: low, scratchy whispers that gave the children chills. You could tell they were getting scared as their eyes widened and they huddled closer and closer together. Meanwhile, Hurricane Alicia continued sending her bolts of lightning that flashed through the windows and her claps of thunder that rattled the walls. *ZAP! BAM! RUMBLE!* The wind began to blow harder as the storm got closer.

Bill described the Hasema woods in terrifying detail as I painted an eerie picture of the graveyard behind the abandoned church where the wild woman lived. There was one kid in particular who was near tears already. Jason pushed his way into the middle of the group, and the look on his face begged us to stop telling the story. But Jason's reaction only fueled us on.

ZAP! Lighting cracked outside, causing the children to jump and gasp. *ROAR!* Thunder followed, pushing the gang closer together. Hurricane Alicia was cuing us to begin telling the legend of the Hasema Wild Woman. In spine-tingling detail I explained:

A family was traveling across the country
during the days of the Old West: a father,
a mother, and a baby girl. Their horse-drawn
wagon rolled swiftly down the old dirt road
when it hit a rock. The collision sent the
baby girl flying off the back of the wagon
and into the ditch by the road. Her parents
didn't notice and the wagon faded away
into the distance.

I paused, and the wind outside began to howl as it wisped through the trees. Lightning flashes flickered off the falling leaves as they blew past the window. *POW!* Lighting cracked again. Bill took over the story at that point. He described:

The little girl laid in the ditch helpless and
afraid in the gloomy fog. Days went by,
and her parents never returned. She was
cold and starving. Then suddenly, red eyes
peered at her through the trees. She heard
growling as a pack of wolves stepped
out of the darkness toward her. Slobber
dripped from between their fangs. Suddenly
the girl snapped back at them with a growl
so chilling that the wolves cowered in
submission. The pack of wolves took her
back to their hidden den deep in the
woods, where they raised her as their own.

At that point, rain was battering against the windows as Hurricane Alicia rolled inland at full force. The children were completely scrunched together on the floor with their backs still toward the windows, frozen with fear from our monstrous ghost story. Lightning flashed and illuminated our faces to look like hollow skulls. I took over the storytelling:

More than a century later, and long past
her death, legend holds that the Wild
Woman still haunts Hasema Road. I said
that her ghost reportedly appears to
victims as a horrifying skeleton of a creature
with pale skin; bony fingers; a creepy
hunchback; long, wiry gray hair; and
nightmarish crimson eyes!

The room was tense with fear — teeth chattering, knees shaking, and goose bumps on top of goose bumps! Bill and I had worked up a bone-chilling, *whopper* of a ghost story. Then we both lifted our heads from the children on the floor in front of us to the windows behind them and, without warning, let out a blood-curdling scream as if we'd seen a ghost outside. *BAHHHHHHHHHH!* Kids flew in every direction like popcorn in a microwave! The most dramatic reaction was from Jason, who jumped up from the middle of the group and dashed off in a mad sprint across the fellowship hall. He screamed at the top of his lungs all the way into the "casino", where the parents were, confessing his sins as he ran!

Bill and I fell off our metal chairs in laughter. Our guts were hurting from laughing so hard, and we clutched our bellies as we rolled on the floor. That is until a real wild woman appeared in the doorway in the form of my mother! Jason stood behind her, whimpering and crying. We were in big trouble! I wouldn't say my mother looked like a horrifying skeleton of a creature that night, but my butt was probably nightmarish crimson. Thunder rolled again. Long lives the legend of the Hasema Wild Woman.

It Was That Dang Red-Headed Preacher's Kid!

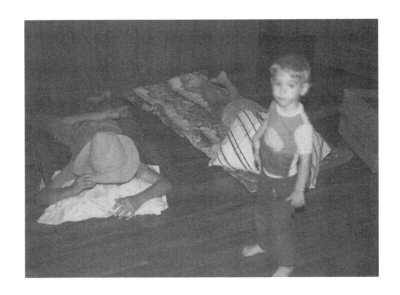

Anyone wanna hear a ghost story?

It Was That Dang Red-Headed Preacher's Kid!

Jim Ed Hardaway

THE SCIENCE CLASS DEBATE

What's not to like about science class? The thought of dissecting slimy frogs and ginormous grasshoppers, or torching up a flaming-hot Bunsen burner is enough to excite any middle-school boy. I couldn't wait to get into high-school science class. Miss H, the teacher, was hot and single, and the crush of every boy navigating the volatile waters of puberty. I would imagine her winking at me during roll call as I responded with an impressive "here" in my newly acquired gravelly voice. But that exhilarating thought would have to remain a part of my daydreams, because I was still in seventh grade and had to tolerate the daily lectures of Mrs. K in physical science class.

Mrs. K had a mound of fluffy gray hair rising high into the atmosphere and thick dark-rimmed glasses that perched on the end of her pointy nose. Her eyes were strangely fierce when she stared at you over the top of those glasses. I remember one day in her class when I got that stare. The bell rang as we scurried to our desk and hurriedly rummaged through our backpacks to pull out our textbooks and Trapper Keeper notebooks. Trapper Keepers made any note taking exciting with their rad themed covers, Velcro closure flaps, sliding plastic binding rings, and assorted pockets for unfinished homework. Unfinished homework was about to become the least of my worries.

The sunlight beamed boldly through the dingy metal blinds, casting thin shadows across the classroom like the lines on notebook paper. A myriad of dust particles swirled in the sunbeams like the solar system, set in orbit by the wind current from the noisy, rumbling air conditioner. It was quite an ironic setting considering Mrs. K's lecture was on the subject of light and darkness.

I knew a lot about light and darkness from my father's sermons on Sundays at our small Baptist church. There are only a few things Baptists love more than glorious light, and that is the Lottie Moon Christmas Offering and potluck socials in the fellowship hall. It was no secret that light was the more popular choice. Choosing light meant a bounty of blessings and the biggest mansion in heaven than you could possibly imagine. I think it's safe to say I was raised with an attitude against all things darkness, and Mrs. K had her work cut out for her if she was going to suggest I embrace it. It turns out that she had other things to say about darkness that piqued my curiosity.

Mrs. K was deadly with a piece of chalk in her hand. Clouds of chalk dust filled the air as she slashed and dashed formulas, theories, and scientific equations across the long, black chalkboard behind her desk. She barked on the effects of light, the speed of light, spectrums, light sources, optics, the visible and invisible, and then, without even stopping to breath—total darkness. Now she had our undivided attention. Lots of cool things happen in darkness like snipe hunting and Sasquatch sightings. But Mrs. K was more focused on what cannot be seen in darkness, like color. She had the audacity to say that *nothing* has color in total darkness. *Uh oh!*

Nothing has color in total darkness? Her comment came as quite a shock to my buddy Bill and me. We could argue with the best of 'em. We were like the dynamic duo of sarcasm, the kings of debating, or as my mother called us—

smart alecks! Bill spoke up first. He tugged on the front of his brightly colored shirt and defiantly replied, "You mean to tell me that this green shirt is not green in the dark?"

Mrs. K's wiry eyebrows tilted in like a dragon as she replied, "Nope, it has no color in the dark." Her hands went immediately to her hips anticipating Bill's reaction.

Oh, this was unbelievable! It's a green shirt. How could it not be green even in darkness? I quickly followed up by grabbing my blue Trapper Keeper notebook. I lifted it in the air and asked, "Is this notebook blue in the dark?"

To this day, I still swear on my grandfather's hearing aids that tiny puffs of smoke came forth from Mrs. K's nostrils as she answered, "I *SAID* it has no color in the *DARK!*"

The rest of the class seemed to know what was about to happen, as they sat motionless in their seats. The air was tense and the debate was on. Bill and I took turns pointing at the most colorful things in the room and quizzing Mrs. K on their appearance in total darkness. Spit was flying! We covered every hue and shade in the color wheel: the primary colors, the secondary colors, and even the complementary colors! Her response was the same with every one: *No! No! No!*

I don't recall if it was Bill or I that uttered the fatal words, but somewhere between electric magenta and hot pink, it just slipped off our tongue: "That's the dumbest thing I've ever heard!" You could hear a pin drop until the piece of chalk snapped in two in the clutches of Mrs. K's hand. She was angrier than my mother the time Mom was cooking sauerkraut and I called it "sour crap." With smoke spewing out of her ears, she pointed at the door and ordered Bill and me to the principal's office. The worst part of the story — Mrs.

K's husband was the principal! We dragged our feet down the long hallway that day, pondering our doom. And, as they say, the rest is history.

Jim Ed Hardaway

VAN VLECK JUNIOR HIGH
REPORT TO PARENTS

Report of _Hardaway, James_ Subject _Science_

School Yr. 19_83_ 19 _84_ Grade _7_

SIX WEEKS PERIOD	1	2	3	Term Exam	Term Grade	4	5	6	Term Exam	Term Grade	Year Average	Credit Earned
Grades	84	78	79	68	80	80	72	66	58	70	75	1
Absent	0	1	0			2	2	2				
Effort	✓	✓	✓			✓	✓	✓				
Conduct	✓	✓	✓			✓	✓	✓				

TEACHER

My science report card... Yikes!

97

It Was That Dang Red-Headed Preacher's Kid!

REMEMBER ALAMO TAPLEY

I loathed English class. Every minute of that never-ending period was a grammatical WWF wrestling match against verbs, verb tenses, punctuation, and relative clauses. Nouns, adjectives, and commas I could handle, but not verbs, adverbs, and semicolons. I probably learned more about sentence structure from playing Mad Libs than I did from paying attention in class.

Our English teacher required us to choose a book from the packed metal cabinet in the back of the classroom, read it by a deadline, and then take a dreadful reading comprehension test. My buddy and I chose the *Sweet Valley High* young-adult romance novels, because the tests were easy—much like the soap opera characters we were reading about. I wasn't allowed to go to school dances because of the profane music and potential make-out sessions, so I had to absorb them from *Sweet Valley High* books every chance I could. We read more of those juicy books than the number of my classmates who wore a single white, sparkly glove like Michael Jackson.

My favorite subject in school was history, and every kid in our small junior-high school couldn't wait to take Mr. M's American history class. Mr. M was a short, dark-haired teacher with big eyebrows who smelled like cigarette smoke. He did a lot of wavy hand motions when he talked and had a way of keeping your attention with his loud and raspy expressions. Rumor had it that he let you watch a full-length movie in his class! What could be better than watching flicks in school? I knew this teacher would be awesome. The movie was a made-for-television mini-series called *The Blue and the Gray*. It was about the Civil War, and it showed epic battle scenes, Abraham Lincoln, blood and guts, and women in ginormous dresses.

I had nothing but good memories from Mr. M's history class, except for the time I farted out loud. That toot ripped out like an armed bank robber with a bag full of loot, vibrated on the wooden desk chair I was sitting on, and turned the heads of every kid in class! I tried to blame it on my friend sitting next to me, but everyone knew it was me because my face turned as red as the stripes on the American flag hanging next to the door. The most feared thing happening to any kid while at school had happened to me, and it was beyond embarrassing. My toot was the hot topic in the lunchroom for weeks, until word got out that sex and private body parts were being talked about in health class.

The history of America wasn't the only topic we discussed in Mr. M's class. We lived in Texas, so the Lone Star State's history was equally important. And you didn't talk about our state's history without mentioning the Alamo. It was the Shrine of Texas Liberty, and as sacred to our state as gold jewelry was to Mr. T! With a piece of white chalk gripped tightly between his fingers, Mr. M whisked his hand around scribbling out timelines and characters on the dusty chalkboard in front of us.

The story goes that on March 3, 1836, under the mild air and cloudy skies of San Antonio, Texas, just over 200 men stood prepared for battle within the walls of the Alamo. Frontiersman Davy Crockett and famous knife maker James — or "Jim" — Bowie were among them. The mission turned fortress was the dramatic stage for an approaching siege that would change the lives of these defenders forever. It was a revolution for Texas's independence from Mexico.

The Texas Army was made up of soldiers, ranchers, craftsmen, and common laborers. Pride flowed through the ranks of this band of brothers, even though the smell of doom was in the air. This small militia was willing to sacrifice their lives for causes they deeply believed in. The cannons were in position. Every man was armed with swords and rifles, and strategic battle plans had been rehearsed. Despite the tireless preparation and determination that carried these men, the daunting reality was that they were no match against General Santa Anna. His Mexican Army numbered in the thousands. Death was certain, but surrender was not an option.

Legend holds that on March 5, 1836, Colonel William Travis gathered his men together for an emotional address regarding the gravity of their situation. He commended their bravery, pronounced his loyalty to his country until his dying breath, and then employed them in their moment of truth. Travis unsheathed his sword and drew a line in the dirt, then assumed position in front of the company. A challenge was presented: all those who were willing to stay and die at the Alamo were called to step across the line and join him in the fight for freedom.

When the line was drawn in the ground, the surge of emotions that enveloped the Alamo warriors was overwhelming. Those men were literally invited to die. Instantly, their minds were flooded with thoughts of family, reflections of home, and fear of death. It was gut wrenching, but there was something stronger rising inside of them. Liberty was calling, on behalf of Texas, and independence was worth fighting for.

When the dust settled from the stroke of Travis's sword, the first man to step forward across the line was Tapley Holland. He leaped across with enthusiasm and pledged his allegiance to Texas. Holland's example inspired the others, and every man in the company followed, except for one. It was a heroic display of honor and courage. Now, here's the cool part of the story — my family is directly descended from Tapley Holland.

Come and take it!

It Was That Dang Red-Headed Preacher's Kid!

UP YOUR NOSE WITH A RUBBER HOSE

Remember those darn things you used to say as a kid? ...That odd array of poetic rhymes you stored deep in the depths of your growing vocabulary and used in word battles? They were sayings like *I know you are, but what am I?* That was one of the most popular sayings because there was always some name calling happening on the playground during recess. Some bully would say, "Is that your face or did your neck throw up?" And you would reply with some weird, quirky smirk on your face: "Stick and stones may break my bones, but words will never harm me!" That was allows a lie. Words hurt and would sometimes leave you paralyzed in emotional trauma.

I'm not talking about bad words either. The bad words were obvious and were never, ever uttered in the presence of any grown-up, even the adults that used bad words themselves. There seemed to be some unwritten law of the universe that allowed grown-ups to spit out profanities like a machine gun without suffering any consequences. I remember one time when my parents left me at my Aunt Carolyn's daycare and, apparently, I unleashed some vile profanity that caused the wind to stop blowing. That resulted in the worst, most disgusting, washing-of-my-mouth-out-with-soap punishment that I ever experienced in my life. I actually think my Aunt Carolyn used a bar of that gritty, lime-green soap that mechanics used to scrub the grease off their hands. *GROSS!*

I grew up in a God-fearing home in the Bible Belt, so when I heard dirty words, it was when I was out in the world among the heathens. That was until my ninth grade year when I myself could cuss the paint off the walls. Saying words like *hell* or *ass* or *piss* was for rookies, because King James said those in his version of the Bible. No, I impressed my friends by inventing cuss words. It was my way of rebelling against the "preacher's kid" label in a feeble attempt to fit in with the crowd. The highlight of the long bus ride home after school was the vile profanities I constructed that left everyone as delirious as Eddie Murphy would leave them. I wasn't into drugs or booze because that was an instant ticket to hell for any upstanding Southern Baptist. At least I still had my priorities straight, right? Profanity seemed like a more forgivable sin. Besides, I wouldn't have known what pot was if you showed it to me and wouldn't have smoked it because it smelled like the very thing for which it was named.

There were more serious words and phrases more hurtful than amusing. I also recall, like it was yesterday, the first time a kid called me a "honky." It was this awkward moment in the second grade when I had left class to go to the bathroom. The kid just stood there awaiting my reply after delivering his proverbial putdown. I had no idea it was a derogatory term, not even a clue. Oblivious, I did what any kid would do in my situation and called him an animal that rhymed with his word: *donkey!* Thank goodness that uncomfortable confrontation lasted all of 30 seconds.

I can remember some of the random insults we would toss around as kids, thinking we were hot stuff. There were times in class when your tongue was hanging out the side of your mouth while your No. 2 pencil etched away at math story problems in your Trapper Keeper notebook. About the time "Billy went to the store and bought 37 apples," you felt someone staring at you. It was always the little curly-haired girl with cooties and no front teeth, so you would look back at her and say, "Why don't you take a picture? It'll last longer!" A good one to use when taunting someone during a feverish game of tag on the playground was: "Nana, nana, boo, boo, stick your head in doo doo!" It was always important to heighten this sneer by putting your thumbs in your ears, flapping your fingers, and sticking out your tongue.

The absolute greatest, my most favorite, and the ultimate clincher of all kid sayings was *Up your nose with a rubber hose!* That was thanks to Mr. Kotter and his rowdy, wisecracking students called the *Sweathogs* from the television show *Welcome Back, Kotter.* I wore that glorious insult out like the tires on my bicycle. *Up your nose with a rubber hose* was the coups de grâce of all comebacks, with stunning results that left hecklers frozen in their tracks! It also came complete with its own tagline that resulted in a final knockout punch: *Up your nose with a rubber hose WHERE THE GREEN GRASS GROWS!*

Getting older meant dropping the childish kid sayings and moving on to single words that showcased one's coolness. I had the extreme honor of being a teenager in the 80s, the greatest decade of all time. We were a colorful group of teenagers. No really, like bright, obnoxious, fluorescent colorful. We wore with great pride our parachute pants, iconic Nike Air Jordan basketball shoes, Polo shirts in pastel colors with the collar flipped up, and friendship bracelets, and we used sensational words like *rad* and *stoked* and *no duh!* We'll talk more about that later. Phrases didn't leave our vocabulary altogether; we just used more mature things like *It's on like Donkey Kong!* or *Yo momma!* Parents even tried to get in on the action by saying things like, "Act your age and not your shoe size!" That was lame. I'll admit it was hard for me to let go of *Up your nose with a rubber hose;* it played such a meaningful role in my adolescence.

Cousins

It Was That Dang Red-Headed Preacher's Kid!

VALLEY GIRL TALK AND SUNDAY SCHOOL PROSTITUTES

When I was five years old, I heard my father preach a sermon on the circumcision of the heart. He referred to the Old Testament where the Jewish males were circumcised. He wisely instructed all the children in the room to ask their parents about the subject when they got home if they had any questions. Well, I had questions, so I brought it up with my parents on the car ride home. That conversation lasted only two minutes because I found out it had to do with my private parts. I threw up my hands in protest and said I didn't want to talk about it anymore. It was funny then, but they had no idea things were going to get worse in my pre-teen years.

The 1980s had its trends and quirks just like any other decade; only its fads were more flamboyant than the others. One of these fads was the Valley girl wave that hit pop culture in the early 80s. It was all about social status and even came with its own California-influenced, materialistic-infused language called *Valleyspeak.* This ditzy slang embraced nasally inflections in phrases such as "like, totally" and "to the max," and emphasized words such as *whatever* and *duh!* Valley girls would also gag over anything they deemed uncool — like fake designer jeans or the geek squad. If a nerd asked a Valley girl to the prom, the Valley girl would say, "Like, *gag* me with a spoon!" or "Feed me cafeteria food and, *like,* watch me throw up!"

111

One evening, our church congregation gathered outside for a fellowship. A *fellowship* is what the Baptists called a social gathering outside of the regular church services. Fellowships included volleyball games, dominoes, secret gossip groups, and potluck meals where the crazy cat lady always brought that weird, unidentifiable dish nobody wanted to eat. Like, *gross!* A small group of us stood behind the sanctuary during the fellowship—my father, a few parishioners, and me. What happened next would forever be ingrained in the hellish lore's of church history.

I don't even remember what it was I wanted or wanted to do. I just know that I wanted it real bad and my father wouldn't allow it. The preacher told me *no!* That deplorable, two-letter word was worse to my kid ears than any four-letter word from a sailor's mouth. I didn't respond to my father's denouncement with a temper tantrum, or even the popular kid response of *why not?* Instead, I reached deep into the depths of my newly acquired Valley girl vernacular I had learned at school and said, "Gag me with a *tampon!*" In case you're wondering, I was completely unversed in the anatomy of the female cycles and had no idea what a tampon was. From the look on my father's face I could tell *like*, he was totally *buggin'* to the max. Like, *duh!* The people next to us just stood there with mortified looks on their faces.

I'd rather not talk about what happened next. I can only say that my father—with his Southern Baptist minister reaction—left no doubt that I had spoken the very words of Lucifer himself. From the look on his contorted face, I had committed the unpardonable sin of blasphemy. Hellfire and brimstone shone in the depths of his retinas! There are no words in the English language to describe his fury that day. I gasped in holy fear as he grabbed me by my pointed red tail and dragged me away to the parsonage to be rendered a heretic. In hindsight, it's quite obvious that I should have used the word *spoon* instead of *tampon*.

This is just one of the many stupid things I did in learning to walk the "narrow way." I was an only child and a preacher's kid. Need I say more? My parents had their work cut out for them. You might also say I was a little sheltered, and facts-of-life kind of stuff was taught to me on a need-to-know basis. This became even more apparent when Mr. H, my Sunday school teacher, mentioned a prostitute.

Sunday school was a short class, divided into age groups, which took place an hour before the main church service on Sunday mornings. I loved going to Mr. H's junior-high class because he was a great storyteller, and he would tell us about his daring adventures if there was time left after the bible lesson. On this particular Sunday, the lesson was from the book of Joshua, in the Old Testament, about the Israelite spies and a woman named *Rahab*. It's here that the reader learns that this lady, with the weird name, was a harlot. A harlot? What's *that?* Well, I asked Mr. H, who thought he was off the hook by telling me it was another word for a prostitute. He wasn't off the hooker just yet, because I had no idea what a prostitute was either. A prostitute? What's *that?*

Silence is loud.

Mr. H sat up straight in his chair, cleared his throat, and proceeded cautiously as he tried to explain to me what a prostitute was without going into too much detail. There were quite a few giggles and wide eyes from the other boys that Sunday morning as they enjoyed the free entertainment. A simple lesson on God's faithfulness turned into an exhaustive dissertation on the world's oldest profession.

There were not any prostitutes in our small town that I knew of, but you can guarantee that I looked at every unsuspecting lady at a street corner waiting to cross the street a little differently.

Flashback to less dramatic times

It Was That Dang Red-Headed Preacher's Kid!

THE HALF-COURT BASKETBALL SHOT

I was the benchwarmer. The long wooden bench that sat alongside our school basketball court was very acquainted with the backside of my small black and orange shorts. I was an energetic eighth grader and as skinny and white as they came. Everything about me worked against my basketball game. My teachers all said I was hyperactive, but my mother called it "energetic." I was undersized at 95 pounds, not the most accurate outside shooter, and even less impressive at the fundamental art of dribbling. Despite my hard-court limitations I was part of the team, the mighty Leopards of Van Vleck Middle School!

It's the faithful duty of every benchwarmer to support the ballers on the court with lots of yelling during the game, and enthusiastic high-fives during team time outs. Every benchwarmer waits for that golden moment when the coach tells them to check in the game and allow a winded starter to rest, even if it's only for a few measly minutes. It's also nice to be creaming the opposing team by 30 points so the benchwarmers can close out the final 90 seconds of the game. The crowd always cheers big-time on those substitutions.

All great ballers have their moment of glory, the Wilt Chamberlains, Michael Jordans, and Larry Birds. These moments happen through evasive steals, epic slam dunks, or game-winning shots. My moment came on a road trip near the end of the season. Our team was crushing the opponent with a comfortable lead early in the third period. The substitution call came. Coach M turned to me with that

117

confident, respected look and told me to check in at the next whistle. Electricity shot through my skinny legs, causing my boney kneecaps to wobble. I was elated, and adrenaline filled my gut as I moved quickly in front of the score table to enter the game. The referee waved me in.

I hustled relentlessly for the first few minutes I was on the hardwood floor, giving pressure on defense, setting picks on offense, and running hard on fast breaks. My final endeavor needed to be a crowd-pleasing shot to prove my worthiness. I made my move on the next possession, when my teammate Joe, we called him *Bulldog,* passed the ball to me to carry down court. With a steady jog, I dribbled forward, took two steps passed mid-court, planted my feet, and shot a 35-foot shot!

In movie-quality slow motion, that orange ball spun through the air. The crowd fell silent as they watched it spiral past the dusty metal lights hanging from the ceiling high above their heads. My lanky arms were frozen in the air in the same position they were when I took the shot. The basketball began its descent toward the basket and slammed against the rim. *WHAM!* I can still hear the echo it created resonating across the gymnasium. After bouncing up and down and back and forth from side to side on the rim, it finally fell through the net with a mediocre swish for three points. I would like to say that the crowd erupted but, on the contrary, everyone was shocked that I attempted such a stupid shot, including my teammates.

After the game, Coach M placed his hand firmly on my shoulder, causing my pits to sweat. His intimidating eyes made contact with mine, burning holes through my pupils. Oddly, a weird sort of smile lifted on the corner of his mouth, and he said, "Hardaway, if you would have missed that shot you'd had a long walk back home!" Then he gave me that signature coach's nod and said, "Nice shot."

It Was That Dang Red-Headed Preacher's Kid!

Jim Ed Hardaway

The benchwarmers

121

It Was That Dang Red-Headed Preacher's Kid!

THAT COVETED NAVY-BLUE CORDUROY JACKET

My arrival on the scene at our small-town public-high-school campus, for my first day as a freshman, was no different than any other all-American teenager. It was the mid-80s, so I am sure there was some form of bright fluorescent colors included in my rad attire, along with my Ocean Pacific T-shirt, black-and-white-checkered Vans, and stonewashed Levi's 501 button-fly jeans. Sure, I may have looked the part, but I was far from fitting in. I kept one eye out for attractive women and the other for hungry seniors wanting to initiate some helpless "fish" like me; that's what they called freshmen in the 80s. So, it's no coincidence that fish traveled in schools, or packs, just like real tuna, mackerel, or cod. There is safety in numbers and shuffling to and fro down the crowded hallways in groups was an advantage against lurking predators hiding behind lockers.

The most feared initiation by any fish was a swirly. That's when a senior holds you upside down over a toilet, sticks your head in the water, and flushes it. For this reason, I never ever went to the bathroom during school. I would just hold it all day and explode when I got home. Most fish took the same precautionary measures, but every once in a while some would try a gnarly move and stray from the pack to relieve themselves. You could always tell who that was because they would show up in the next class with a wet head, a pale look on their faces, and in desperate need of some cologne and a comb. The seniors weren't that patient though. Their preferred method of initiation was dropping a fish butt first into a trashcan. This move left the fish stranded helplessly with their hands and feet sticking out the top of the trash can into the air, and their butts smushed to the bottom against only-God-knows-what.

I remember my buddy Korey getting trash-canned before science class one day. For some odd reason, he decided to flirt with danger and taunt an upperclassman. We saw the movie *Back to the Future* that summer, so I'm guessing Korey thought he was Marty McFly and this guy was Biff Tannen. As you would expect, "Biff" and his gang quickly snagged "Marty" and hauled him kicking and clawing to the nearest waste receptacle and disposed of him. We all had a great laugh at Korey's expense that day. A plutonium-powered DeLorean time machine was just what he needed to go back in time and erase that humiliating incident.

Our freshman year was a long and painful one. I spent most of it scrambling to finish my Algebra homework on the morning bus ride to school or hiding in the shadows for fear of my life. This behavior was not very effective when trying to pick up chicks; that had to be put off until my sophomore year. But there was one class that brought us all together. When we stepped across the threshold of our ginormous and beautifully brown agriculture building, the chains of disunity seemed to fall off. At that moment, we were not upperclassmen, nerds, jocks, preps, or even fish; we were all Future Farmers of America!

To be a Future Farmer of America was the totally righteous gig at our high school. We called it "FFA" or "Ag" class. Don't ask me why it was so popular; processing deer meat and identifying breeds of cattle were not high on my list of notable hobbies or skills. I was in to collecting Star Wars action figures and ninja throwing stars, but FFA was

124

my ticket into the "in crowd." That coveted navy-blue corduroy jacket with the huge, glowing, mustard-colored FFA logo on the back was where it was at! It even had my name embroidered on the front in impressive cursive lettering, which proved to upperclassmen that my name was not fish. There were all kinds of things I could have been involved with in FFA besides messing with animal guts or changing tractor tires, and I chose to be on the Chapter Conducting Team.

Chapter conducting is when teams compete against other schools to demonstrate their knowledge in correct parliamentary procedures. At competitions, teams are given scenarios and asked questions about parliamentary law. There were gavels, "ayes" and "nays," amending, voting, and appealing. It was rather cheesy I might add, but our Junior Chapter Conducting Team took third place at the District III competition in 1985, quite an accomplishment for this kid who probably had a Yoda action figure in his pocket for Jedi wisdom.

What I remember most about FFA was the infamous nail box. The nail box was a large wooden box overflowing with every sized nail imaginable: box nails, finish nails, drywall nails, long nails, short nails, rusty nails, and fat and skinny nails. There was at least a gazillion nails in that box! Our Ag teachers, Mr. O and Mr. P, created the nail box as a horrible punishment. If you got in trouble for something, they would make us kneel in front of it on the hard concrete and fill a coffee can with certain kinds of nails. Process a deer foot through the sausage grinder and you'd get the nail box. Make sensuous faces while milking a cow and you'd get the nail box. In my case, I was goofing off during chapter-conducting rehearsal. You guessed it—Mr. O caught me and sentenced me to the nail box. He told me to dig for eight penny nails until hell froze over! I was a preacher's kid, so I knew I'd be digging through that box for a really long time. That year was my one and only as a Future Farmer of America, but I got to keep the jacket!

Sketch of the trash-canning incident

It Was That Dang Red-Headed Preacher's Kid!

SCHOOLYARD SCUFFLES

It was one of the strangest brawls I had ever seen in all my years as a student in the public-school system. Tension had been brewing all day between two of my classmates, Tommy and Chet. Trash talk, pushing and shoving, and nasty verbal threats led to a head-to-head match after school.

I don't remember why they were so mad at each other. All I know is that they wanted to rip each other's faces off! They crossed paths throughout the day, staring each other down and talking smack about who was going down after school. Confrontations and chest bumps happened in the cafeteria, in the gym, in the library, and in the hallways between classes. Chet had his band of brothers with him all day, a group of troublemakers who acted like they wanted a piece of the action too. I don't think they were sticking up for him; they just wanted to see a good fight. Tommy had his following too, and I was one of them, and I can tell you for a fact that's all *I* wanted to see.

The final bell rang and reverberated through the school. We poured out of the building like the Israelites through the Red Sea, in a mass exodus to assemble for the duel. I was in the group behind Tommy, and across the parking lot came Chet and his gang. We walked across the street to an area in front of an apartment complex. Everyone made a circle around the two fighters to form a makeshift boxing ring.

There were at least a 100 students there. Talk spread through the spectators as to who would win the fight, and there may have even been a few bets placed on the side.

129

Some hecklers chattered at Tommy and Chet, trying to egg them on. The fighters exchanged some crass words and a slew of obnoxious profanities, the kind of words that get your mouth washed out with soap if your Aunt Carolyn were to hear. The fight was on!

You won't believe what happened next.

I think it is safe to say that Tommy outweighed Chet by at least 30 pounds. It was like a Rottweiler against a Chihuahua. Tommy and Chet began dancing around with their fists in the air like Sugar Ray Leonard and Thomas Hearns! After a few preliminary shoves and missed swings, Tommy drew his fist back and punched Chet square in the left eye. *POW!* You could feel the reverberation as the crowd gasped. It was a direct hit! Chet swaggered back and forth like a drunken sailor then fell straight to the ground. *THUD!* He immediately grabbed his eye in pain and surrendered to his opponent. A one-punch knockout and this fight was over.

Talk of the fight spread like wildfire the next day at school. Tommy wore a gladiator's smile, spreading his broad shoulders with pride and relishing in his victory. Chet wore sunglasses and hid in the shadows, but nothing could hide his huge, swollen, black eye. Neither one of them had anything to be proud of.

I had that terrible feeling in my gut, one I had felt before.

The year before, I had been in my own fight. The concrete basketball court, in the field behind the middle-school cafeteria, was the hot spot during lunchtime. The boys were all on a quest to become the next Michael Jordan, so we would cram down our meals and then race out back to get first dibs on a pickup game. I usually got there late and had to settle on watching the game in progress—hoping that the bell wouldn't ring before I got my turn. The only other option was to join a violent game of dodge ball with the maniacs at the red brick wall of the gymnasium.

I think I was still chewing my food when I ran onto the basketball court, but I was there first. A few of my friends were close behind, and we quickly put together a game of three-on-three hoops. We were well into our game — dribbling and shooting around — when Freddie ran onto the court and interrupted our game. He grabbed the ball away and petitioned us to re-pick teams and start over so he could play. I was so mad my eyebrows crinkled! The conflict began. I got in Freddie's face and told him to give us back the ball. He stiffened his chest, got in my face, and asked me what I was going to do about it. I thought to myself: *What would Daniel LaRusso do?*

Daniel LaRusso was a teenager from New Jersey in the hit movie *The Karate Kid.* It was one of my favorites. Daniel and his mom move to Reseda, California, in her beat-up station wagon, to start a new life. He is invited to a beach party where he meets a cute blond girl named *Ali.* He soon finds out that she is the ex-girlfriend of Johnny Lawrence, the menacing leader of a group of karate punks called the *Cobra Kai.* The Cobras thrive in harassing LaRusso and making his life miserable. Daniel finds hope in his apartment complex's maintenance man, a good-natured Okinawan named *Mr. Miyagi.* The two form a close friendship and Mr. Miyagi trains Daniel in karate, teaching him to control his hot temper and avoid fighting whenever possible. LaRusso and Lawrence face off at the *All Valley Karate Championships,* leading to the climactic ending when Daniel defeats his rival Johnny with the Miyagi-inspired crane kick.

I had no time for a crane kick or for any Miyagi training. Freddie, intent on taking over, was breathing hot air in my face. So, I used my pushing skills, gritted my teeth, and gave him a hard shove. *WHOOSH!* Freddie recovered and pushed me back. *WHOOSH!* The other guys moved in closer, expecting to see a fight. I couldn't turn back, so I clinched my shaky fist and took a swing at Freddie. *BIFF!* I connected with his jaw and then braced myself for the inevitable. Freddie reacted with a quick swing to my left cheek — *BAM!* Pain shot through my delicate face from my chin to my earlobes. We both just stood there staring at each other in surprise for what seemed like an eternity, realizing that neither one of us wanted any part of a fight. Coach M noticed the scuffle from a distance, ran over, and called off our 30-second bout. That was it. The only fight I had in my entire life equaled two pushes, two punches, and some spit-flying insults. From that day on, I happily embraced my role as a lover and not a fighter. Mr. Miyagi would have been proud of me. Freddie and I were friends ever since.

Mr. "T"enacious?

It Was That Dang Red-Headed Preacher's Kid!

BEETLE MISCHIEF

The boys cocked their arms back as far as they could and hurled the water balloons through the air. Laughter quickly followed as the colorful H2O bombs hit their target. *WHAP! SPLAT! POW!* A carful of my friends had just nailed an unsuspecting jogger running beside the road. But it was no ordinary jogger; it was an off-duty police officer! *Busted* is such a miserable word, and miserable is what my pals felt as they took an unplanned trip to the city jail and had to call their parents to explain what had happened. A good prank must *always* be tactical and well executed, including a worthy objective, clear assignments, and most important, an escape plan.

It was the mid-80s, and we had one thing on our minds: high-speed trash-can tipping! That's when we'd drive by trash cans at high rates of speed, knocking down as many as we could all over town. The garbage trucks had them emptied by breakfast, and we'd have them tipped over by lunch. This time we had our sights set on the large plastic trash can sitting by the street curb in front of our school principal's house. My friend Jamie gripped the steering wheel and revved the engine of his 1972 Volkswagen Beetle, pumping the gas pedal with his foot as he flashed a mischievous grin my way in the passenger seat. He was the driver, so that meant I was the tipper. I stretched my arm out the window like the wing on a Boeing 747, ready to smash the trash can over when we drove by. Jamie floored it and the rear tires of his baby blue VW Bug spun into action, as they spit gravel and dust high into the air behind us. I leaned further out the window, and my mullet waved in the wind like the mud flap on an 18-wheeler. In the nano second my fist hit the trash can, I realized it wasn't empty but completely full, so it wouldn't budge. Our principal must have filled that thing with ready mix concrete or something! My arm flew backwards from the impact, slamming hard into the metal window frame and sending shock waves of pain down my spine! I winced in agony, rubbing the back of my arm and my throbbing triceps. Jamie couldn't stop laughing as we zoomed away.

I know what you're thinking, that we were mischievous and asking for trouble. And you'd be correct about the mischief, but trouble we wanted no part of. Something peculiar happens in a teenage boy's brain that no scientist, or doctor, or father has ever been able to successfully diagnose. The doctor might say the medulla oblongata is still developing. The parent might say it's a form of brain damage. Mothers tend to blame it on puberty while fathers label it as idiotic, moronic, or just plain stupid. I can't deny that all of this may be true, but the fathers are probably the ones who hit the proverbial nail on the head.

We executed the common pranks with precision and triumph... Things like tipping trash cans, wrapping houses with toilet paper, and backing through drive-through windows to order fast food. But these things got boring, so we moved into the adolescent phase of inventing our own pranks. Jamie had the '72 Beetle, and I had a '79 Honda Prelude. That thing had more rust than Van Halen had hit songs, but it did have a super cool trunk hatch release just below the driver's seat. So, we rigged a handle on the trunk lid where it could be closed from the inside and put Jamie in there. We'd drive through town—on main streets and in parking lots—popping the trunk at ideal spots like stoplights or crowded shopping areas. I'd pull the lever, and Jamie would pop up, scream, or bark at innocent pedestrians and then slam the truck lid back down as I sped away. We laughed so hard at people's reactions! It would either scare them half to death or leave them smiling and shaking their heads at our ridiculous behavior. I would like to say that our pranks ended there, but it got worse.

Adult grocery-store clerks were trained to give teenage boys the evil eye when they arrived at the checkout stand carrying several dozen cartons of eggs, knowing full well they were not planning ahead for the community Easter egg hunt. And I am ashamed to tell you Jamie and I weren't, in fact, doing our civic duty to donate eggs to the community. We were going egging, so it was more like "delivering" chicken grenades to the community.

It was getting dark when Jamie sped down side streets as we hurled eggs at mailboxes and other nameless targets. *SPLAT! SQUISH! KA-POOSH!* Tires squealed and laugher filled the car. It was all fun and games until we kicked it up a notch and decided to egg the row of parked cars near the center of town. Heaven help us, we had just egged the fine patrons of the First United Methodist Church! Jamie downshifted the Beetle and quickly disappeared around the next corner.

I condensed the remaining eggs into one carton and then tossed the empty cartons onto the rear floorboard. We started looking for our next target when, without warning, a pair of headlights flashed in the rearview mirror in hot pursuit! An angry egg-covered Methodist began chasing us through the narrow streets, flashing his headlights and pounding on the horn. It was no exaggeration—we *panicked!* Jamie reacted with a quick jerk into gear and pushed the pedal to the medal. The Beetle's 1600 cc air-cooled pancake four-cylinder engine launched us dangerously fast through the neighborhood—weaving through potholes, swerving around parked cars, and taking sharp last-second turns. No wonder the Methodists beat us to the buffet line at the pizza joint after Sunday morning services. Our pursuer thought he was Mario Andretti!

We burned rubber for several blocks, and the chase seemed to last for an eternity. Speaking of which, I repented at least 100 times for fear of spending mine burning in the lake of fire! Finally, we lost Mario in the billowing smoke of a city mosquito-spraying truck while our hearts pounded from the hysteria! Jamie and I just looked at each other in shock as he steered the Beetle onto the main highway leading out of town. *Did Mario get our license plate number? Could we be identified in a criminal lineup?* I needed a change of underwear!

We ended up at our school basketball practice at a gymnasium several miles away. My Uncle Gary, who was an assistant coach, was also a county sheriff! I expected him to get a call at any moment, cuff us, and haul us off to the slammer. Our prank days were temporarily suspended for fear that we might not make it into heaven, and I came to the short conclusion that I liked my eggs scrambled instead of splattered.

The pranksters

It Was That Dang Red-Headed Preacher's Kid!

THE FREESTYLIN' SUMMER

Finally, I had pulled it off! I was standing up in the air like a surfer on my BMX bike—my arms spread out like a hawk—with one foot on my seat and the other one on the handlebars. That's what the old school flatland freestyle trick was called in the 80s, a *Surfer*—BMX is short for *bicycle motocross*. I can't tell you how many times I busted my skinny you-know-what, trying to learn that trick in the parking lot behind the church. My foot would slip off the handlebars or I didn't have enough speed, and I'd lose my balance trying to stand up and crash to the ground. My audience was the cackling buzzards perched on the electric power lines above me. We called them the county sanitation department, and I must have looked tastier than the flattened roadkill roasting on the hot asphalt of nearby Highway 457.

When I was younger, I remember pedaling my bicycle as fast as I could. I sat crested on the banana seat of my gold and orange bike, gripping the oversized handlebars for dear life. Underneath me—fastened snug in the heavy-metal frame—was a bright red racing plate with the bold white number 65. My legs pumped up and down on the pedals of that machine like pistons in a V-8 engine, and my excessively round bowl-cut hairdo blew in the wind. I was just a pint-size American kid, and from the moment I lost the training wheels on my first bicycle, I was shredding the back roads of Texas.

Growing up, I had groovy bikes with chopper-style handlebars and race plates, and ones with gas tanks and

141

fenders like a motorcycle. Until 1985, my stunt portfolio consisted of jumping off warped pieces of scrap plywood—propped up on shaky stacks of cinder blocks—like stuntman Evel Knievel. Well, kind of like Knievel. The cars I was jumping over were my Hot Wheels cars lined up side by side on our dirt driveway. Now I was pulling off ramp tricks, gut levers, surfers, endos, and even making up my own tricks—like "The Crane" inspired by *The Karate Kid*.

A new family started attending our little country church. They had a kid my age named Dewayne, and we started hanging out. He was into surfing, skateboarding, and BMX bikes, and I quickly took an interest. He showed me a few freestyle bicycle tricks, and everything changed. We'd go to the mall, and I would hit the bookstore to get the latest issues of *Freestylin'* and *BMX Plus!* magazines. I begged my mom for a stylish haircut and took down all the Bigfoot Monster Truck and Ferrari posters from the walls of my bedroom. They were replaced with pullout posters and page cutouts of freestyle bike riders from the magazines.

Those mind-blowing freestylers were radical! There was Eddie Fiola who rode GT Bikes, Mike Dominguez who rode a Haro, and the greatest of all time and my favorite rider, Ron Wilkerson. Even the way they talked was cool. They used words like *stoked, rad, tubular,* and *bitchin'*. My vocabulary changed overnight, and it wasn't uncommon for me to say *rad* in every sentence. I exhausted these words on a daily basis, except for *bitchin'* around my parents of course. Even though *bitchin'* meant "cool" my mom would've had coronary failure, and the preacher would've exiled me like John the Apostle!

Ron Wilkerson's Haro bicycle was that "word" I didn't say around my parents. His fluorescent-colored threads, thrilling tricks, and highly coveted bike were too hip. Wilkerson's ride had high-end gear like a hollow bolt freestyle stem, fork pegs, and Skyway Mag wheels. It was designed to shred hard-core. My ride was the crappy, low-end Huffy bike with a chain guard and reflectors from the local discount store. It was designed to ride around the block and make your mother smile since she knew you were safe. Sometimes I'd look up and see her smiling and waving at me through the kitchen window. I needed to get legit fast!

I saved every dollar I earned during the summer of 1985 — mowing the church lawn and picking up pecans from the trees down by Caney Creek to sell. As soon as I had enough money, I'd go to the bike shop and buy a new GT part to upgrade my Huffy. One of the shops was *Sonrise Bikes & Boards*, owned by this rad surfer dude named *Steve*. My friend Dewayne worked for him at *Sonrise* for a while, repairing bikes and selling surfboards. I rebuilt my Huffy one piece at a time. Johnny Cash would've been proud. It wasn't long until I had a bike that could hold up under the freestyle tricks I was learning, and it was bitchin'! Uh, I mean, rad — it was *rad!* The freestylin' summer was one of the best, but it wasn't just the BMX bikes that made it so unforgettable.

Something magical happened that summer that captured our generation's attention, from the Goon Docks neighborhood in Astoria, Oregon. *The Goonies* invaded movie theaters, taking us on a magical journey. The Goonies — Mikey, Chunk, Data, and Mouth — hang out for one final weekend before developers tear down their homes. The guys rummage through a dusty, cluttered attic and discover an old, tattered map leading to "One-Eyed" Willie's pirate ship and hoards of hidden treasure. Mikey's older brother, Brand,

and two girls, Andy and Stef, stumble into the quest as well. With the help of a Spanish Doubloon, the Goonies find themselves in a swashbuckling adventure — running from the villainous criminals, the Fratellis, dodging booby traps, confronting skeletons, and befriending a deformed monster named *Sloth*. The Goonies take viewers on a roller-coaster ride through underground tunnels and falling boulders and down rapid water slides. I felt like I was a part of it all, right into the cavern lagoon where they discover Willie's derelict pirate ship and treasure room full of gold!

The Goonies taught us more than Chunk's dance called the *Truffle Shuffle;* they showed us what true friendship is all about. They taught us to take risks for passionate causes and to live like there's no tomorrow, because Goonies never say die! The movie also taught me a little bit about romance — how an unlikely guy from the Goon Docks, Brand, could end up with a popular girl and cheerleader, Andy. I actually caught myself enjoying a good kissing scene. What in the world was happening to me?

Freestylin'

It Was That Dang Red-Headed Preacher's Kid!

THE RAD GIRL WITH THE BIG HAIR

Puberty does strange things to teenage boys. To think that they would even consider, for a moment, getting rid of their vast toy collections for a girl is insane. I never imagined there would be a place in time when I had to think about trading in my Princess Leia in her slave outfit action figure for a girl, or driving a car instead of riding my bike. An intruder called *testosterone* arrived on the scene dressed in a velour sweat suit, and his business card read: *Voice-Changing and Hair-Growth Specialist*. There was also a bunch of embarrassing fine print I'd rather not repeat.

My multi-zippered, synthetic nylon parachute pants used to touch the ground, and then suddenly the stripes on my sports socks began showing. I spent more time battling acne in front of my bathroom mirror than pretending to be Indiana Jones on an archaeological expedition in the woods down by Caney Creek. But it would be a miracle if I could even get a date with my face covered in ungodly amounts of Oxy10 — a cream designed to hide and combat pimples.

It was my sophomore year in high school when I found out she liked me.

It was noon in the noisy school lunchroom. My friends and I sat around a wobbly folding table, rummaging through our lunch sacks to pull out our smashed sandwiches, bags of chips, and Little Debbie Snack Cakes. The conversation was shallow as we scarfed down our food. We rambled on about girls, BMX bikes and skateboards, girls, what movies we wanted to see on the weekend, and girls.

147

That's when something caught my eye.

I looked up to see a short, curly-haired girl at the table across from me. She was waving her hands back and forth in the air, trying to get my attention, and grinning from multi-pierced earlobe to multi-pierced earlobe. Once she made eye contact with me, she began pointing to the girl seated in front of her. As she pointed, she mouthed the words, "She likes you!" It took a few seconds of her repeating her actions for me to catch on to what she was saying. When I finally caught on, I looked down at the girl she was talking about. It was the hottest woman in school, and there was no way I believed her. This had to be some cruel joke. I had to be dreaming. I thought to myself: *Was this for real? She likes me?*

The whole scene played out like a cheesy episode of *Square Pegs*, but for me it was momentary bliss. Her name was *Tonya*, and she was drop-dead gorgeous. She was a brunette with big brown eyes, a beautiful face, and a mesmerizing smile. *Wacka-wacka!* And did I mention her enormous, rad hairdo that split the clouds as it soared high into the heavens? It was as fluffy as the clouds it pierced. She had to use just as much White Rain, extra-hold hair spray as I did Oxy 10! I was a total dweeb with a spiked haircut, zits, excessive peach fuzz on my upper lip, and a permanent sunburn — the complete opposite of tall, dark, and handsome.

One thing led to another, and I eventually asked Tonya to be my girlfriend at a friend's party. I was so nervous that my Right Guard deodorant was working hard to fight back the sweat building up in my armpits. We were standing on the balcony overlooking the apartment complex's swimming pool. To us, it was like an ocean view. The synthesizer pop sounds of Duran Duran played through the stereo in the party room. The moment was so awkward that she answered

148

yes and then rushed away to tell her friend — the short, curly-haired girl who started it all. Tonya left me standing there, hungry like a wolf and alone with a ridiculous grin on my face. I'm pretty sure my facial expression is why the other guests made a mad dash for the punch bowl, thinking the bubbly lime-green punch inside of it might've been spiked.

It sounds sappy, but I wanted to be with Tonya every second of every minute, of every hour, of every day. And yes, I did use the classic setting-the-watch-back trick when my parents set a curfew. She was worth every bit of the trouble I would get into when I finally did make it home. I knew that one day I would marry this girl, and we'd have a Stryper song played at our wedding. I couldn't get enough of my Tonya, so when we started working together it was even more sublime.

Our first jobs were at a local grocery store called *Safeway*. My buddy Jamie worked there too. Jamie and Tonya were both cashiers, and I was a sacker. In vivid, slow motion, I watched her beautiful hands scan grocery items and then send them down the conveyor belt so I could put them in the sack. Fluorescent light beams gleamed off her teeth as she flashed me that gorgeous smile. That was the best job in the world! When I sacked for Jamie, I was grabbing a catcher's mitt because he was lightening fast and hurled groceries through the air like Nolan Ryan throwing baseballs to Alan Ashby! *Be careful with the eggs — not the eggs!*

Jamie and I managed to stir up mischief whenever we had the chance. If we weren't in his Beetle, knocking over trash cans in town, we were locking our co-workers in the dairy cooler at the back of the grocery store. We'd sit on the outside of the door laughing as our victim — trapped inside — would bang his fists on the same door and begging for us to let him out. Sometimes we chose to be on the inside of the dairy cooler ourselves because it was a great place to pull pranks on customers. A shopper would stroll down the line, on the outside, looking at the yogurts, butter, and milk products. From the inside, we'd watch and wait for them to pass by, and then we'd push out a can of yogurt so it would fall on the floor behind them. It never got old as we would watch each poor customer look around trying to figure out had happened.

Our inspiration came from Mr. A, the store's crazy old pharmacist. From where he stood in the pharmacy, he could see straight down the aisle to the meat market. When a customer reached over to grab a package of ground beef, Mr. A would pick up the store intercom, moo like a cow at her, and say, "See how fresh that beef is ma'am!" That shopper would quickly pull back, grinning and looking around everywhere to see who the culprit was. Mr. A would laugh and wait for her to reach for the meat again. For some reason he also got a kick out of yelling, "boppity bop" at us when we walked by his pharmacy to get to the stockroom.

Even with fun-filled workdays at Safeway, I couldn't wait to get the weekly schedule to see what time I had off during the weekend. My minimum-wage paycheck burned holes in my pockets, and the mall or the beach was always calling my and Tonya's names. Getting to those places put the need for some wheels even higher on the priority list. A teenage boy needed a car more than Mike Tyson needed speech therapy.

When I was a teenager, my dream car was a Ferrari. This is why I loved watching the television show *Magnum P.I.* I didn't tune in because Thomas Magnum was a private investigator with a killer mustache that lived in Hawaii; it was because he zoomed onto a crime scene in his bright red Ferrari 308 GTS! The reality of owning the Italian super sports car one day was simply unrealistic; especially on my minimum-wage salary as a grocery sacker at Safeway. So, I had to dream smaller and wish for a Pontiac Fiero. The Fiero was a two-seater, mid-engine sports car with energetic styling like its hero the Ferrari. It was not as exotic. For that, it was sometimes called the "poor man's Ferrari." If a poor man could afford a Pontiac Fiero, that meant I was flat broke.

My friend's sister had a black Fiero, and she let me drive it to the mall one time. I felt a little like Magnum, pulling up to the mall that day, minus the flashy Hawaiian shirt and the epic mustache, of course. His 'stache was like face furniture, a masterpiece lip rug. For the moment, I would have to settle for my rusted out '79 Honda and pubescent peach fuzz. But, I didn't care, because my rad girl with the big hair thought both were cool, and all was forgotten when we were together.

It Was That Dang Red-Headed Preacher's Kid!

That rad girl!

It Was That Dang Red-Headed Preacher's Kid!

MALL MANIA AND THE COUPLES-ONLY SKATE

I was a big Michael J. Fox fan in my teen years. I tried hard to enjoy drinking Pepsi Free like his character Marty McFly did in the movie *Back to the Future,* and I begged my mother to buy me sport coats with elbow patches like his character Alex Keaton wore in the television show *Family Ties.* So, it was no surprise that I loved going to the mall to scope out the latest toys, novelties, fashion, and gadgets—hoping that I would stumble across a real Mattel hoverboard to ride to school or some self-lacing Nike Mag shoes for the basketball court.

A mall is compiled of numerous retail stores all side by side under one ginormous roof—clothing stores, variety stores, specialty and department stores all coming together at the food court. Each store contributed to the unique smells of synthetic materials and fast-food grease, blended together and funneled throughout the building, courtesy of the air conditioning system. Mall mania reached the pinnacle of radness in the 1980s. It was the place to go and shop, explore, play, browse, and covet. It was also the place to go if you had nothing else to do, or when you simply wanted to loiter and put out the vibe. The trips I took to the mall came in waves, during eras in my life I can associate with friends and experiences.

The earliest exploits I had at the mall were with my friend Chip. Our families hung out often, and we had been friends since we were little tikes. Our parents told us that Chip would scream bloody murder when he was upset and I

155

used to say, "Shut up, *Chipper!*" But Chip got his revenge because he would always push me over just to see me fall. Our families took trips together to the Houston Astrodome to watch demolition derbies or baseball games, and even took a Colorado vacation once to stay in a mountain cabin and go snow sledding.

The sledding hill had a riding trail right through the middle of some tall, snow-covered spruce trees. It was really steep and fast, so our dads built a three-foot snow barricade at the bottom of the run to keep us from going into the street. On one particular run, Chip lost control and came flying down the hill faster than Richard Petty at the Daytona 500, sending rooster tails of snow soaring high into the air from the blades of his sled. We all watched in dismay as he blasted down the hill and right through the barricade. *SMACK!* Snow went flying everywhere, and he came to a sudden stop in the muddy ditch on the other side. *CRASH!* That was our painful cue to retreat to the cabin for some hot chocolate by the fireplace.

I remember some rad things Chip had in his room when we were older—like an Alex Van Halen poster, Stop Thief game, and a plastic Spider-Man piggy bank jammed full of pennies. There must have been a gazillion dollars in that web-slinger bust that he could exchange for tokens at the video arcade in the mall. That was always the first place we'd go to get our fix on Defender, Tron, Pole Position, Joust, and the Midway classics, Galaga and Ms. Pac Man.

We stepped into that dimly lit arcade called *Yesterdays* — our pockets bulging with quarters—to wage wars on centipedes, space invaders, enemy knights on flying ostriches, and Blinky, Pinky, Inky, and Sue! The vibrant incandescent marquees across the tops of the black video arcade cabinets added a splendid glow to the buzzing atmosphere. Digital bleeps, zaps, chirps, laser blasts, and explosions were music to our ears. That mysterious electronic-burn smell permeated our adolescent senses until there was nothing left in our pockets but wads of lint. When the final, dreadful words *Game Over* flashed repeatedly on the screen, we'd leave and make the rounds to the other mall hot spots. Next, we needed some fuel for our precarious growth spurts, so we'd grab a quick snack to stop our unruly stomachs from growling; at least momentarily.

Chip always tried to talk me into going to a Mexican-food restaurant called *El Chico* to get some chips and salsa. He devised a cunning plan to sit down and only order water to drink. Since the chips and salsa were complimentary, we could get a free meal and then make a quick exit when the waitress wasn't looking. I must confess it was a brilliant plan, but I was chicken so we settled for some waffle fries at Chick-fil-A. With snack in hand, we headed to JCPenney to see if the Atari Game Center was open for play. If there was a long wait, we'd pop into Sam Goody to browse through the cassette tapes, and then over to KB Toys to choose a Star Wars action figure or toy we'd beg our parents for later.

The mall also housed a plethora of temptations, where boys could tangle themselves in a web of transgressions if they weren't careful. Right across from the toy store was a specialty shop called *Spencer's*. Its window displays were deceptive, showing products like Halloween costumes, movie-themed T-shirts, and Rubik's Cubes. But beyond the threshold, it was stacked to the ceiling with every vile perversion and corruptive, risqué novelty item imaginable! Chip and I would look both ways to make sure our parents were nowhere in sight and then make a mad dash into

157

Spencer's. We were always terrified of coming out of the store and running right into them. Of course, we only went in there to look at the blacklight posters. *GULP!*

Those were good times, which ironically, was one of my favorite afternoon sitcoms on television. I would watch *Good Times* every day after school and can still hear skinny J. J. Evans, who would be wearing his signature navy-blue hat and flamboyant smile, scream, *"Dy-no-mite!"* when he was excited about something. Cruising around the mall was "dynomite." It was more thrilling than going through puberty while trying to sing in the youth choir, when my voice crackled back and forth between a low rumble and a high squeaking shrill.

The next eras of mall trips were more intentional. I was a teenager so my appearance and name-brand products were top priority. Strapped to my hip was my most prized possession — my bright yellow Sony Walkman cassette player. I never went anywhere without it and even had the sports, waterproof version so I wouldn't have to take it off in the shower. Music was a huge part of my life, and my dream of becoming a drummer in a rock band demanded that I look the part too. Although I desperately wanted a Huey Lewis and the News T-shirt, I knew that the preacher wouldn't allow it, so I filled my wardrobe with Ocean Pacific shirts.

Town & County Surf Shop was the place to go. It was also a great place to grab wax for our surf and boogie boards. The most popular brand was called *Mr. Zogs Sex Wax*. Getting caught with anything deemed "sex wax" meant eternal damnation. If I felt like being a rebel, I'd sneak it. My friend Dewayne was braver than me, so he'd buy Mr. Zogs and tell his mom that was all they had available when she ragged about it. The last thing I wanted to be was a "Cletus."

That's what we called a looser, dweeb, or lame-o. But most of the time, I'd play it safe and buy Bubble Gum Surf Wax instead.

The absolute best trips to the mall were with my girlfriend, Tonya. We'd hold hands and never let go as we shuffled among packs of other teenagers dressed in Guess, Member's Only jackets from Chess King, leg warmers, Vans shoes, Polo shirts, Jordache designer jeans, Contempo Casuals sweaters with the iconic padded shoulders, and Reebok high tops. We liked wearing these black canvas Kung Fu shoes with brown rubber soles, so we'd go into the Asian imports store and get matching pairs. One of our favorite stops was the jewelry department in Dillards, where we'd check out the latest Swatch Watches. They weren't just watches; they were vivid, new wave-inspired, totally rad accessories. If you were a trendsetter, you wore multiple neon Swatch Watches on one arm. Tonya and I both had several Swatch Watches, and we were always shopping for the next one to add to our growing collection.

Not far from the mall was another popular hangout called *Skating America.* It was an indoor roller-skating rink. Our church youth group — along with other area churches — would show up for "Christian Youth Night." This was a special night giving churches a discounted admission rate and offering hours of roller skating to the righteous, synthesized, pop sounds of contemporary Christian music. I assumed the rest of the week was open to secular music, debauchery, and all kinds of worldliness.

The parking lot was packed full of every 15-passenger van and repurposed school bus in the county. There was the brand-new van with shiny, chrome wheels from First Baptist Church parked next the banged-up hoopty van with balding tires from the non-denominational church. There were always puffs of smoke coming out from under the hood of that one.

Everyone showed up for "Christian Youth Night" at Skating America—from the United Methodists to the Pentecostals, except for the Independent Fundamental Baptists of course. Any gyrating of the hips; music with raw, distorted guitars; or the potential for teenagers of the opposite sex to bump and grind was strictly forbidden. In all fairness, we had our share of annoying adult chaperones too. They watched us like hawks from the filthy concession-stand booths on the side of the rink, and they were quick to call out any provocative activity. Most of them were parents of teens themselves, and we didn't get more than a few finger shakes before our names called out. But, inevitably, there was always the grumpy, heavyset lady from church who hated teenagers but, for some reason unknown to mankind, insisted on volunteering for youth group trips anyway.

After lacing up our signature Skating America roller skates with the beige boots, orange wheels, and worn-out toe stop, we'd hit the glossy hardwood floor and start making laps. There was nothing like a bunch of heaven-bound teenagers skating around in circles, shaking their money makers to the tunes of Michael W. Smith, Petra, DeGarmo & Key, and the greatest of them all, *Stryper!* This heavy-metal, glam-rock regime took Christian music to an entirely new level, by breaking through to mainstream with songs like *Soldiers under Command* and *To Hell with the Devil.* They also pushed the limits with their yellow-and-black-striped spandex costumes, big hairdos, and thick eyeliner. Stryper's lead singer, Michael Sweet, invented octaves by splitting the airwaves with his distinctive high-pitch screams, and the drummer, Robert Sweet, redefined coolness by calling himself the "visual timekeeper."

The Skating America disc jockey kept rockin' the holy hits while sporadically jumping on the mic to tell us to skate backwards, change direction, or to announce the highly anticipated couples-only skate. This was the moment when all the chaperones panicked, the heavyset volunteer lady cracked her knuckles, and our youth pastor spilled his soda jumping up from the table to try and stop it. It was his worst nightmare, but it was too late.

The house lights dimmed and the disco ball—dangling from the ceiling in the middle of the building—started to spin slowly. Its brilliant, crystal rays danced around on the walls throughout the room, cutting through the darkness with its glimmering light beams. Stryper's popular rock ballad *Honestly* began to play. The single people slowly exited the skate floor, and all the couples joined hands in a romantic stroll around the rink. My girl took my hand, and we joined in, hoping that song would never end. We sped up when passing the adults and then slowed back down on the opposite side of the rink, hoping to sneak a kiss or two in that shamefully dark corner where the one fluorescent light fixture was always broken.

We skated in circles until our socks were sweaty and we had blisters on our feet. The heavyset volunteer lady wore a hole in the musty carpet near the entrance, pacing back and forth while staring at the clock on the wall. An annoyed door attendant weaved a vacuum cleaner around her, trying to finish his closing duties. The final song played and the house lights brightened. We turned in our skates and shuffled out the exit door to pile in the vans and buses. Everyone pushed and shoved to claim the disreputable back seats. Once seated, my girl leaned her head on my shoulder as our hoopty church van sputtered out of the crowded parking lot and down the highway. I rewound my thoughts and played back the evening's couples skate like the mix tape in my Sony Walkman — over and over again.

Colorado adventures

It Was That Dang Red-Headed Preacher's Kid!

BORN TO RERUN

I laid there on the football field with my face mask buried deep enough in the turf to smell the blades of St. Augustine grass. My hands gripped the football tightly against my chest as the referee blew the whistle, to signal the play dead. Our opponent had just kicked us the ball, and I caught it. Instead of running, I just fell on it. I rose to my feet to a silent crowd, puzzled looks from my teammates, and the bellowing growl of my angry coach. His voice parted the air like a militant Moses parting the Red Sea, sending shock waves of disgust from the sidelines to my ears. "Run with it, *Hardaway!* Don't *fall* on the #@% ball! *Run with it!*"

It was embarrassing.

I was a starting wide receiver on the eighth-grade football team, but small enough in stature to pass for a seventh-grader. So my coach illegally played me and another kid on both teams, because we were athletic and fast. I thought to myself, *This is a seventh-grade game I'm playing in, and Coach is chewing me out for a bad play?* My temper began to flare the more I thought about. *I'm not even supposed to be playing in this game! You're a cheater and you're yelling at me?*

When I reached the sidelines Coach grabbed my helmet and continued to scold me. That did it. I had had enough, and I wasn't going to play victim to his scrutiny. So I quit. On the bus, after the game, I just told my coach that I was quitting the team. I let my emotions get the best of me, and I was disappointed in myself when the realization hit that I was a quitter. *All he wanted me to do was run. If only I had a second chance.* Turns out I did get a second chance, an opportunity to "rerun," if you will.

Coach turned off the county highway and drove our cross-country team down a bumpy, gravel road. It was early on a Saturday. We were headed to our first cross-country track meet of the year to race against the other schools in the district. On either side of the road were aging barbed wire fences. Our bodies swayed back and forth with the motion as we weaved our way through the woods, dodging bumps in the road and kicking up fallen tree branches and rocks. The road debris made erratic, loud popping noises under the fender wells. Coach followed the dust cloud from the car in front of us until we a reached a clearing where others were also arriving. We parked in an open spot and got out of the car.

I nervously adjusted the orange sweatbands on my wrist, sizing up our competition as our team walked toward the sign-in table among the other contenders. It was intimidating for us freshmen, since we had no experience to go on. Coach told us to find a spot and start stretching while he got us checked in. Danny and Grant were sophomores who already had a year of races under their belts, or in this case, their elastic waistbands. My friend Korey and I annoyed them with repeated questions for the next 20 minutes, trying to get a better picture of what to expect in the race.

Cross-country was long-distance running in the great outdoors. Some races were held on school campuses, but the ideal ones were out in the country over natural terrain. This particular meet was a two-mile course through the woods — the route was marked with neon-orange flags on the oak trees. For me, these open-air courses were the best motivators. I could imagine myself being chased through the forest by an angry, rabid wolf with drool dripping from its enormous fangs. Only this time, the wild canine would be the kid from our rival school the Bulldogs, with leftover Pop Tart crumbs on his lip from breakfast.

We stretched our quads and calves until Coach rejoined us with instructions on the matches for the morning. The freshmen races were first, so we immediately made our way over to the starting line. There were about 30 kids in our heat, so winning the race would be a big challenge. The odds were against me, but I soon found out they were the ones I had foolishly created for myself rather than the number of competitors surrounding me.

It was springtime, so during the weeks leading up to that first meet our high-school football stadium was busy with track-and-field athletes practicing baton relays, throwing shot puts, jumping over hurdles, and pole-vaulting during our seventh period athletics class. Coach had the cross-country team training long distance on the road leading out of town. Each day, our orders were the same: suit up, lace your shoes, and run to the railroad tracks past Roselawn Cemetery, and back to the school before the final bell rang. That allowed us roughly 45 minutes to accomplish a three-mile round trip that took at least an hour to walk.

It was too much running for my buddy Korey and me. We would jog off the school grounds with the group and down Fourth Street, until we reached the bridge at the edge of town. There we ditched the pack and hid under the bridge. We'd wait down there and goof off—busting littered glass bottles or skipping rocks across the slough—until we heard the group returning back. Then we'd emerge up the steep hill to rejoin them and run back to the school. The other runners would smirk and shake their heads each time, but surprisingly, they never snitched on us.

Skipping rocks on the water doesn't help runners win races, and I was about to learn that the hard way. I elbowed my way to the front of the group and took a deep breath. The runners leaned forward as the starting gun fired into the air. *POW!* Everyone jolted ahead—most in a sensible, steady pace but a few stupid ones in a full-blown dash out in front. I was among the latter. My legs were pumping, my arms pulling. We ran out of the open field and into the woods.

The heat was so intense that sweat began pouring from my skin in a matter of seconds. I jumped over a fallen tree. Every breath was a chore as my lungs begged for more oxygen. Only a few contenders were ahead of me, so I was in the top five and distancing myself from the herd of sprinters behind me. My throat was dry, my tongue parched. I ran down a steep embankment and through a dry creek bed with cracks in the dirt like veins, and I forced myself up the hill on the other side.

That's when things began to change.

The glory of being in front was short-lived. Not even half a mile into the race—with a mile and a half left to go—I began slipping farther and farther back. My muscles ached; my chest heaved with every stride. One by one, runners passed me up. The pain in my body kicked in fast—the wheezing and the throbbing lending to my physical dilemma. The earth beneath my shoes felt hard and unforgiving, like an angry judge sentencing a criminal. It was evident that I was guilty of being a slacker, not preparing for cross-country racing like I should have.

By the time I reached the finish line, I was completely exhausted and walking. The senior-citizen mall walkers would've passed me up. Only a handful of runners finished after me, but there was no honor in my performance and nothing to celebrate. It was humiliating. The more disciplined runners ran with a steady pace that day, and my teammate Danny was among them.

There was a lot to think about over the weekend as I nursed my wounds. Let's be honest, the option to quit was even on the table. Then I remembered that day on the football field the year before, when I stopped playing the game I loved because of a stupid decision. It sucks living with regrets. Fortunately, there was enough achiever left in me to not give up again. I knew what had to be done, and it was going to cost me something.

Danny's mom was my English teacher and his family went to our church. So, I caught up with him during seventh period one day as we jogged out of the athletic field house towards Fourth Street. It was challenging to keep up with his pace. Running beside him, I asked how he got to the railroad tracks and back so effortlessly every day. I'll never forget what he told me. He told me that he didn't think about running to the railroad track; he thought about running to the bridge. Yea, the same bridge I would hide under and bust bottles. When he got to the bridge, then he thought about running to the dead armadillo on the road 50 yards ahead of him. Then it was the John Deere tractor sitting in the pasture by the highway, then Roselawn Cemetery, and before he knew it, he was touching his shoe on the steel rail of the tracks and turning around to run back to the school. As Danny was explaining his method, it began to click. It was so simple, yet clever. He was setting smaller goals to reach along the way, and in doing so, he was methodically succeeding in the bigger goal at the same time.

I had nothing to lose, so I gave it a try. I'll admit that it wasn't easy because it was still a long way to run in a short amount of time. The dead armadillo baking on the hot pavement was a bit disgusting too, but I held my nose and pressed on as I jogged by. Each day, I repeated the process, becoming more disciplined. My body was getting into shape. Props to Doug E. Fresh and Slick Rick's rap hit "Ladi Dadi" that played in my Walkman as I ran. Those tricky rhymes helped me keep pace and took my mind off the burning muscles.

There was an unexplainable exhilaration in accomplishing those small goals, and I soon discovered they renewed my energy. Since athletics was the last class period before school was out, I got an idea. I told my coach about it and made sure it was okay with our school bus driver. The next day, I took a handwritten letter from my parents to school, a letter giving me permission to keep running past the railroad tracks to see how far I could get on the way home before the school bus picked me up.

Athletics class finally came at the end of the day. I suited up, double-tied my dusty shoes laces for the long run, and then headed out. The bridge, roadkill, and John Deere tractor came rather quickly. I think the farmer who owned that yellow and green tractor found out it was our goal marker and got a kick out of parking it farther and farther each day. Soon after, I sprinted past the cemetery and those legendary railroad tracks. After that, there was a whole new world of targets to aim for—a derelict combine, the buzzard sitting on the speed-limit sign, the bright yellow crop duster at the municipal airport, and the faded Lone Star Beer can in the weeds.

I had run over seven miles when the bus pulled over to pick me up near Wildcat Slough. The bus driver opened the doors and flashed me a smile when I climbed aboard. As I made my way down the narrow aisle past the jittery elementary and junior-high kids—the high-school kids always sat in the back—I was greeted with jovial cheers of elation and accolades of high fives from my fellow classmates. They were shocked I had made it so far.

While that first cross-country race had almost 30 freshman runners in the heat, the starting line I stood at later had only three. There were two rival Bulldogs and me. And rather than a scenic race through the woodlands, this course sprawled out over the Bulldog high-school campus in a small town not too far from ours. I was in enemy territory. The odds were stacked against me again. My adrenaline was pumping; I could feel my heart pounding against my puny chest. The official raised his pistol in the air and fired the starting shot. *BANG!*

My two opponents blasted off the starting line and quickly distanced themselves ahead of me. I established a pace and set my first visual goal. One Bulldog barreled ahead of his teammate to take the lead. We ran across an empty parking lot, running across yellow line after yellow line, and then took a long, curved turn behind the chain-link fence of the baseball stadium. Although I was in last place, I ran with more confidence, but it was still grueling. Along with the steady pace came that familiar pain in my lungs from the heavy breathing. They pumped like pistons in an engine. I'd like to say that engine was a gas-guzzling V-8 with a roar, but it was more like a road-weary 4-cylinder rust bucket with a weird, knocking sound. We ran behind the south end zone of the football stadium, took a sharp turn,

171

and then went underneath the metal bleachers on the side. The short stretch of shade was a welcomed relief from the raging sun firing heat waves at us from the sky. Sweat was pouring.

A long stretch of open field stood between the stadium and the halfway point; its dry, scorched grass provided little cushion under my feet. The marked course around the campus was only one mile, so we would make a second lap to equal out the two-mile race. That halfway point would become the finish line next time around. It was strange watching the two competitors in front of me make the same dumb mistake I made in my first race. Gradually, the second Bulldog runner lost his steam and I slowly passed him up nearing the first mile. I swear he growled and snapped as I went by, but it was probably just my imagination. A few students stood along the side whooping and nagging him on, but it was not enough to revive his fatigued haunches. He was dog-tired — pun intended.

There were just two of us left as legit contenders in the final one-mile lap. I passed another goal by jumping over the busted curb of the parking lot. The distance was shortening between the front-runner and me, not so much from a change in his pace but from the extra energy I had from maintaining mine. When I reached the fence behind the baseball field, he was just 20 yards away. It was my moment of truth. Suddenly, it hit me that I could win this race. There was just enough time and distance for me to make a move and take the lead. We ran past the south end zone of the football stadium and turned underneath the metal bleachers. The thought of defeating these two rivals on their own turf was invigorating. I pictured myself running across the finish line first, with my arms stretched up in victory formation. That simple muse was like kerosene on a campfire.

Somehow my aching legs felt it too. I ran hard out from under the football stands and into the long stretch of open field. The first Bulldog had been looking back at me the entire race, checking his lead. This time, he turned his head around and saw a skinny, albino Leopard hot on his heals! My muscles went numb from the exertion; my heart pumped blood in its own race through my veins. Dust from the field stuck like grit to the back of my dry throat. Parents and students pushed closer to the finish line as we approached. The crowd cheered. I could see my coach and teammates standing on one side. The banners waved.

Bulldog and I were shoulder to shoulder in a mad dash. My will *begged* my tired body for power like Milli Vanilli pleading for forgiveness over the lip-syncing scandal. The driving guitar sounds of Joe "Bean" Esposito's "You're the Best" song, from *The Karate Kid* soundtrack, echoed through my head. There was no stopping, no giving up. The official bent over in movie-like slow motion. His chubby hands rested on his sweaty knees, and his squinty eyes peered down the white chalk finish line painted on the grass. A striped tube sock streaked into his peripheral vision and across the line first. The sock was mine—I had won the race. It was the biggest victory since Ronald Reagan defeated Walter Mondale in the race to the White House.

*   *   *   *

As you've read through the pages of this book, it's quite obvious to you that I'm a big kid who carries a lot of great memories with me from my childhood years. I can't help it;

I'm just a nostalgic kind of guy. In saying that, I want to fully acknowledge that not all of the recollections from our childhoods are the best. In fact, there may be some you've experienced that are pretty ugly and painful, haunting ones you'd rather forget but they always seem to claw their way back into your thoughts at the worst of times. I can assure you that I experienced a few of these as well.

Excluding the bad memories from these pages was my intentional way of denouncing their robust potential to influence my destiny—a healthy denial of sorts. Remember, no person, no "thing," and no circumstance has a right to define you. Don't let bad memories charge you rent for your thoughts; evict them by paying tribute to the good memories.

When did our lives become predictable and ordinary? What locked away your imagination? Don't you feel it too, that tugging at your spirit to dream again? Set your imagination free. Let your mullet down and choose to be unconventional. Travel to fantastical places, journey, and discover again. Never be afraid to take risks, to face your fears, and to embrace humility. It may, at times, leave you vulnerable and exposed. It will require you to be open and honest with yourself, to be true to the passion in your heart. It may even require you to stop wasting time under the bridge and start running again. You were born to rerun, just like that dang red-headed preacher's kid.

¡Adiós!

The bridge

It Was That Dang Red-Headed Preacher's Kid!

It Was That Dang Red-Headed Preacher's Kid!

Check out the free downloadable resources
for book clubs and small groups at
www.DangPreachersKid.com